LOST LANES

36 GLORIOUS BIKE RIDES
IN SOUTHERN ENGLAND

JACK THURSTON

LOST LANES

CONTENTS

THE RIDES
MAP

Cambridge

22

21 ■ Baldock

25

20 ■ Stevenage ■ Braintree

Aylesbury ■ Harpenden ■ Harlow ■ Chelmsford

Oxford ■

High Wycombe

Swindon ■ Didcot 17 16 L O N D O N Gravesend

Reading 29 28

18 Windsor 6

10 30 1 Rochester

Woking 13 Sevenoaks

Basingstoke 12 ■ Reigate 2 Maidstone

Andover ■ 11 3 Tunbridge Wells

Haslemere Crawley 7

Winchester ■ Horsham

14 8

Southampton ■ Brighton Hastings

Portsmouth 9 ■ Chichester Eastbourne

15 Isle of Wight

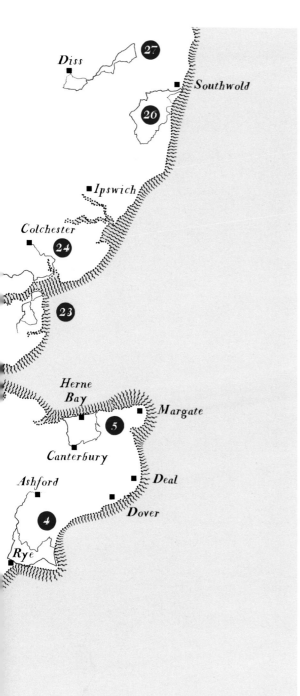

No.	COUNTY	NAME	FASTEST TRAIN FROM	START / END POINTS
1	Kent	Valley of Vision	Victoria	Swanley
2	Kent	Houses & Hills	Charing Cross	Sevenoaks
3	Kent	Between Downs & Weald	Victoria	Lingfield
4	Kent	The Fifth Continent	St Pancras	Ashford
5	Kent	Crab & Winkle	St Pancras	Canterbury
6	Kent	The Loneliest Landscape	Charing Cross	Gravesend/Strood
7	Sussex	The Wild Weald	Charing Cross	Tunbridge Wells
8	Sussex	A Quintessence of England	Waterloo	Liphook
9	Sussex	Turf & Surf	Waterloo	Chichester
10	Surrey	Windsor Great Park	Waterloo	Egham
11	Surrey	Surrey Hills Legbuster	Waterloo	Effingham
12	Surrey	The Ripley Road	Waterloo	Woking
13	Surrey	Everything Stops for Tea	Victoria/Waterloo	Westhumble
14	Hampshire	Winchester Winter Warmer	Waterloo	Winchester
15	Isle of Wight	Around the Wight	Waterloo	Ryde
16	Berks/Bucks	Escape to Cookham Island	Paddington	Iver/Slough
17	Berks/Oxon	A Thames Meander	Paddington	Reading/Didcot
18	Berks/Oxon	River to Ridgeway	Paddington	Reading
19	Oxfordshire	A Cotswold Getaway	Paddington	Long Hanborough
20	Hertfordshire	Chiltern Rendezvous	King's Cross	Harpenden
21	Hertfordshire	Hidden Hertfordshire	King's Cross	Knebworth
22	Bedfordshire	Farmland Fantastic	King's Cross	Baldock
23	Essex	Empty Essex	Liverpool St	Southminster/Burnham-on-Crouch
24	Essex	The Oyster Run	Liverpool St	Colchester/Witham
25	Essex	Joy of Essex	Liverpool St	Elsenham
26	Suffolk	Sun, Sea & Suffolk	Liverpool St	Dunwich
27	Suffolk	Waveney Weekender	Liverpool St	Diss
28	London	An Eastern Excursion		Broadway Market
29	London	Garden City		Lambeth/Soho
30	London	Wimbledon to Weybridge	Waterloo	Wimbledon/Weybridge
31	Essex/Suffolk	Dunwich Dynamo		Hackney/Dunwich
32	Kent	Ride of the Falling Leaves	Victoria	Dulwich
33	Hertfordshire	Summertime Audax	King's Cross	Stevenage
34	Essex	Foulness Island Bike Ride	Liverpool St	Great Wakering
35	Surrey/Sussex	London to Brighton		London/Brighton
36	London	Midsummer Madness		London

MILES	KM	ASCENT(m)	TERRAIN	GRADE
22	36	437	Mostly quiet lanes with a brief section of off-road track	Moderate
32	49	595	Quiet lanes and one well-surfaced cycle track	Challenging
29	46	473	Quiet lanes	Moderate
63	101	299	Mostly quiet lanes, a few stretches of busier roads	Easy/Challenging
32	51	249	Quiet lanes and well-surfaced cycle paths	Moderate
30	49	221	Quiet lanes, a couple of busier B-roads and a well-surfaced cycle track	Easy
37	58	917	Mostly lanes and B-roads, with a short section of railway path	Challenging
38	60	624	Quiet lanes and one short, optional off-road track	Moderate/challenging
27	44	43	Quiet lanes and unsurfaced tracks	Easy
15	24	189	Surfaced paths and a few quiet suburban roads	Easy
46	74	1296	Country lanes, with short stretch of busier road	Very challenging
20	32	145	B-roads out of Woking, then quiet lanes, optional canal towpath	Easy
23	37	240	Quiet lanes, with one section of unsurfaced track	Easy
39	63	632	Quiet lanes and surfaced cycle paths, one section of main road	Moderate/challenging
68	109	1048	Quiet lanes, a few short stretches of busier main roads & riverside path	Moderate/challenging
32	51	157	Riverside paths, country lanes, woodland tracks and a few urban roads	Easy
35	57	357	Riverside path, quiet lanes	Moderate
30	48	339	Mostly lanes; a few sections of unsurfaced track	Moderate
66	106	1124	Quiet lanes, with two stretches of A-road with cycle lanes	Moderate/challenging
43	70	507	Quiet lanes, a couple of short sections on main roads	Moderate
37	60	586	Quiet country lanes, short bridleway to reach ruined chapel	Moderate
35	56	195	Mostly lanes, quieter B-roads and two short sections of off-road path	Moderate
28	44	62	Quiet lanes, a few miles of of unsurfaced track	Easy
39	63	149	Country lanes and a few stretches of B-road	Easy
38	62	243	Quiet lanes with a few short sections of B-road	Moderate
44	71	180	Country lanes with a few sections of off-road track	Moderate
48	77	183	Quiet lanes with a short section of B-road	Moderate
21	33	37	Canal towpath, surfaced cycle tracks and a few quieter urban roads	Easy
14	22	119	Traffic free paths and quieter London streets	Easy
19	31	104	Well-surfaced off-road paths, some quiet suburban roads	Easy
112	180	1189	Busy urban roads leaving London, then B-roads and country lanes	Very challenging
62	100	950	Urban roads leaving London, then country lanes	Very challenging
63	101	520	Country lanes and a few quiet B-roads	Moderate
23	37	43	Traffic-free lanes and one track	Easy
54	87	709	Urban roads leaving London, B-roads and country lanes	Challenging
12	19	116	London streets at night	Easy

IN SEARCH OF

LOST LANES

—

According to statisticians, southern England is the most crowded part of pretty much the most crowded country in Europe, and a look at a road map reinforces that impression. At the centre, London, an urban octopus whose tarmac tentacles reach out far into the home counties. Beyond the M25, a dense constellation of ever-growing towns. Year by year, ring-roads, retail parks and industrial estates eat further into England's green and pleasant land, concreting over the countryside. At least, that's how the story goes.

But there's another story, of a magnificent and surprisingly tranquil countryside. From standing stones on windswept hilltops to bluebell-filled ancient forests, from sparkling chalk streams to lazy rivers, flower-filled meadows to unspoiled beaches, bustling harbours to neat village greens; for natural beauty and human history, this is the equal of any place in the world.

That southern England is so heavily populated makes it all the more satisfying to seek out its hidden corners and wild places, whether that be a thousand-year-old fresco in a tiny Saxon church, a meadow dotted with marsh orchids or a sun-kissed swimming hole.

And it's not all the remnants of a mythical pastoral idyll. There's grandeur and elegance in the pylons that stride across the Chilterns. The offshore wind farms of Kent add a new dimension to the luminous seascapes that enthralled Turner and Conrad. Spending a summer night on top of the Sinodun Hills in the upper Thames Valley and watching as the first light of day fell on the monumental cooling towers of Didcot's power station is as close to a spiritual experience as I can remember.

TRAVELLING AT THE SPEED OF THE LAND

This book is based on my belief that there is no better way to explore southern England than by riding a bicycle along its 'lost lanes', the quiet capillary counterparts to the network of thundering arterial roads. These strips of serenity represent as much as a third of the road network by length, but carry just a tiny fraction of the motor traffic. Lanes classed as 'generally less than 4m wide' are perfect for cycling for the simple reason that most motorists shun them. They're too narrow for cars to pass each other without slowing to a near halt or backing up to a passing place; not knowing what's around the corner, those people who do have to use them drive slowly and carefully. It's an ideal environment for cycling.

All the rides in this book are accessible by train, which is both faster and less stressful than driving to them. Cars have their uses, and more than 80 per cent of the people who ride bikes also own cars, refuting overblown claims of a factional war on the roads. Even so, taking a car 'detox' for a day or two – or more – is good for our own sanity as well as an act of spontaneous kindness towards other cyclists. And this is just where the benefits begin. Of all modes of travel, only the bicycle combines freedom and speed with total immersion in the surroundings: the sun, wind and rain, and every sight, sound and smell. As Ernest Hemingway said, 'it is by riding a bicycle that you learn the contours of a country best'; we don't just see the landscape, we actually feel it, sweating up hills and freewheeling down them. Lost lanes might not be the quickest or most direct route from here to there, but nobody sees the world better by going faster.

LIFE ALONG THE LANES

Lanes are fantastic places for nature. The hedgerows that line them are often ancient, and many owe their longevity to their roadside position. There has been little incentive for farmers to grub them up, unlike the hedgerows that divide fields. Lanes pass through all kinds of land, from pasture and meadows to ancient woodlands, coppice, heath and scrub. Their hedgerows and verges are green pathways and a lifeline for wild flora and fauna, some of which can be eaten. And it's more than just blackberries: pick elderflowers for cordial, wild garlic for a novel twist on pesto, and later in the year sloes for sloe gin or chestnuts for roasting.

The story of our country lanes, capped by just a thin veneer of tarmac, is the story of Britain itself, from long-distance drovers' roads that date back to the Bronze Age, to flat, straight Roman military roads and medieval pilgrims' trails. Most common of all are the simple tracks between farmsteads, which for thousands of years have seen nothing of note but the unremarkable to and fro of daily life. Yet over the years these everyday journeys have literally worn themselves into the texture of the land: dark 'hollow ways', their high banks overgrown with snaking beech roots, or the chalk scars across the downland are testament to countless feet, human and animal, that have travelled the same way. Cucumber Lane, Bread and Cheese Lane, Dig Dog Lane, Sheepwalk Lane – curious names, each with its own story to tell. These are the lanes that the journalist and social reformer William Cobbett rode on horseback in the 1820s, writing about what he saw in his famous *Rural Rides* and asserting that 'those that travel on turnpike roads know nothing of England'.

LOVE YOUR LANES

The rides in this book wind their way through the very best of the countryside, on quiet roads, lost lanes, off-road paths and tracks, always striving to follow the ways least travelled. Towards the end of the book, I've included a handful of the best organised group rides, because sometimes it's fun to ride with a crowd.

One aim of this book is to rekindle a passion for Britain's lost lanes, and this rich network offers endless opportunities for improvisation. No two bike rides are ever the same, even if they follow exactly the same route. I hope you enjoy riding the routes in this book and building upon them by devising your own variations. Becoming a cycling connoisseur of lost lanes can be summed up in three steps.

First, discover your lost lanes. Get out the Ordnance Survey maps and look for the thin yellow lines. If you're not familiar with the symbols for the castles, churches, wildlife reserves, tumuli and the like along the way, it can really help to get to know them. For a real bird's eye view, go to *twomaps.com* and explore the twinning of map and aerial photography.

Next, get to know them. Identify the wildflowers and come back a couple of months later to see what's changed. Listen to the birdsong, name the trees. How are the bees and butterflies doing? What's growing in the fields beyond?

Finally, and above all: just ride. At any speed, in all seasons, for the thrill of the new or the comfort of the familiar. Alone or with friends, pack a picnic or stop at a pub for lunch, bring a towel and go for a swim, have a snooze under a tree, take some photographs – even write a sonnet if the mood takes you. Savour the beauty and wildness of these perfect threads of common ground and celebrate the very best way to see them – by bike.

Jack Thurston, *London, 2013*

HOW TO GET STARTED

Ensure your bike is in good mechanical order. If in doubt, take it in to your local bike shop for a basic service covering brakes and gears. If you're new to cycling or haven't ridden for a long time, start with the easy rides before moving on to the moderate and challenging ones. There are some practical tips at the back of the book, starting on page 250.

LEAVE THE BOOK AT HOME

This is a weighty book and the last thing anyone would want to do is carry it around for a day's cycling. That's why all the information needed to ride the routes is available for download from the *Lost Lanes* website. Listed at the end of each ride is a web page where you can view a more detailed map and download a paper route sheet or a track for navigating with a GPS device or smartphone app. Alternatively, use the sketch maps in the book to trace out the route on good paper map, such as the Ordnance Survey's incomparable 1:50,000 Landranger series.

BEFORE YOU GO

TOUR D'HORIZON

—

In 2012, London saw the Shard topped out as the new highest building in Europe. From the top, on a clear day, it is possible to see for 40 miles. It's a view that takes in most of the biggest landscape features of southern England, the features that shape the rides in this book.

To the east lies the Thames Estuary, wide and silvery, the tidal river commingling with the waters of the North Sea. The delta shoreline of the Thames comprises pan-flat marshes, mudflats, islets and creeks. They can be forbidding places, the sites of abandoned military installations, heavy industry and the occasional forlorn caravan park. The wildlife seems indifferent to the starkness of it all, and these are some of the best places to observe seabirds, both year-round residents and migratory species. There are spots along the Thames where a sense of the river's long history as the starting point of seafaring adventures still hangs in the air, as well as pretty sailing and fishing villages.

South of the Thames lies Kent, the gateway to the British Isles for travellers from the continent and a county with as much variation as any in England. What the cyclist notices first about Kent are the hills, which can be brutal. But there is a softer side to the county, in the flatter lands around the cathedral city of Canterbury or between the Downs and the Weald. This is traditionally the 'garden of England', where orchards are filled with blossom in the spring and early summer, and fields of tall poles spill with fragrant hops later in the summer. At Kent's southern tip lies the shingle spit of Dungeness, an alternative Land's End, clinging to Romney Marsh and – unlike much of the low-lying eastern coastline – growing in size rather than slowly succumbing to rising sea levels. Dungeness is a wild, windblown spot that's full of character and rich in history.

The North Downs, a steep chalk ridge, stretch from Dover's white cliffs to the Hog's Back near Farnham in Surrey. The hills are crisscrossed by innumerable lost lanes and, for the cyclist prepared to venture from the road, many more unsurfaced tracks and bridleways. Further south, running from Beachy Head near Eastbourne to Winchester in the heart of Wessex, are the South Downs, southern England's first and only National Park. The South Downs are shorter and marginally lower than their northern counterparts, and have fewer roads, but they offer even grander vistas. Each range of hills makes for fine cycling, if a little strenuous at times. In gently undulating West Sussex and Hampshire the countryside becomes ever more lush, the villages ever more delightful. The geological strata of the southeast converge on the Isle of Wight, the sunniest county in Britain, where the landscape has a little of everything: a rugged southern coast with cliffs of chalk and sandstone, a rolling interior and a low-lying northern coast fringed by marshes.

To the west of the capital, the Green Belt has somehow failed to contain the urban sprawl, and the busy roads of suburban Metroland make carefree cycling harder to find. Rivers and canals are the saviours, their banks offering leisurely rides in quiet surroundings, though there are some lovely lanes to be found, particularly when the road turns uphill into the western edge of the Chilterns. Beyond Reading is the very first scent of the west country, particularly among the Berkshire Downs, a ridge composed of the same mass of chalk as the North and South Downs and the Chilterns, which stretches uninterrupted towards Avebury and the sacred landscape of Salisbury Plain. The upper Thames valley is a lazy, gently rolling landscape of

Sussex Weald

historic towns and lovely villages, with windmills dotting many of the hills. Beyond Oxford lies the idyllic landscape of the Cotswolds, in all its golden-hued glory.

The landscape to the north of London, in Hertfordshire and Bedfordshire, is less hilly and a little less dramatic than that to the south, but it is by no means flat. Much of it is fertile arable country – this is where the East Anglian plains begin – and despite quite a number of large towns, there is plenty of good cycling country to be found. Further east the landscape is flatter, the riding is easier, and each village in north Essex is more lovely than the last. Just beyond lies Suffolk's cluster of stunning medieval towns and villages, whose giant churches and half-timbered houses tell of a time when the wool trade made this the wealthiest place in England.

READING THE LANDSCAPE

You don't need to be a geologist to grasp the basic changes in the underlying landscape as you ride. A look at the buildings, particularly the older ones, can be sufficient because until very recently, builders have tended to use whatever local stone is available. Thus what has been built above the ground is a good indication of what lies below.

On a ride from Oxford to the Essex coast, the warm, honey-coloured limestone of the Cotswolds soon gives way to red brick made from the gravel and clay deposits of the Thames basin. Crossing the Chilterns, it changes again. The white, crumbly chalk is the crushed remains of tiny creatures that lived in the tropical sea under which Britain once lay. It is studded with flint – hard, glassy lumps of rock that have been used heavily by both Chiltern and Downland builders. Sometimes it is combined with other materials into a rough kind of rubble, but for churches and the homes of the well-to-do, the flint is split to reveal a single flat face and carefully arranged into geometric patterns. In Hertfordshire and Bedfordshire brick is back on the menu, and sometimes local sandstone. Essex is a county that lacks a ready supply of stone, and for many hundreds of years wood was the material of choice. The older timbered buildings of Essex and

Suffolk have walls infilled with wattle-and-daub and decorated with ornate pargeting, or sided with overlapping wooden planks, the latter to protect against corrosive salt blown in from the sea.

To anyone with time to look carefully at subtle changes in the landscape from one place to another (and who better than the touring cyclist?), the countryside is more than a book to be read; it's a whole library containing history, arts, economics and the natural sciences. It's not just the building materials that change, but the styles of architecture that vary by place and by period. Churches are the most obvious manifestation of local distinctiveness: the round towers of Suffolk, Norman arches carved with zigzag patterns, the tall shingle spires in Surrey and Sussex and the small, squat chapels of the South Downs. Besides being places of worship, churches are also an almost unbelievable repository of art and craft. I'm not religious, but I will happily take a detour to look at a thousand-year-old wall painting or an exquisitely carved marble font. Viewed *in situ*, these works are many times more powerful than when seen in a sterile museum. Most churches leave their doors open or display instructions on where a key can be borrowed.

The geology and climate of each area also determine the opportunities available to those who make a living off the land. The uplands of the Downs and the Chilterns are grazing country, too poor or too steep for growing crops. They are perfect for wildflowers, and the early summer displays on the Berkshire Downs and the South Downs can be breathtaking. The lowlands are more fertile and more intensively farmed, with vast fields devoted to arable monocultures of wheat, barley and oilseeds; in the sunniest, most fertile places of all, market gardeners grow vegetables and fruit. Where the land is so low as to be prone to flooding, it is turned over to pasture for dairy cows and beef cattle. Modern farming has wrought profound change on the countryside, most of it for the worse, but there are also nature reserves and well-managed woodlands, and many farmers are now paid to do conservation work on their farms. Some of the most beautiful and appar-

ently 'natural' landscapes are in fact not natural at all, but totally reliant on grazing livestock, without which they would revert to scrub and bracken.

As one of the most heavily populated and most intensively cultivated parts of the world, there is precious little true wilderness in southern England. Yet there is still plenty of wildness and wildlife, as animals and plants find niches in fields, forest, marsh and heath, much of which is now protected by law or in nature reserves. Immune to our aesthetic prejudices, wildlife inhabits neglected man-made sites too; these in-between places, dubbed 'the unofficial countryside' by the nature writer Richard Mabey, 'edgelands' by the environmentalist Marion Shoard, and 'brownfield' by dismissive politicians, can be ecologically valuable and possess their own curious and unexpected beauty.

RIDING THE SEASONS

Nature reveals itself most abundantly to those who 'ride the seasons'. Starting in February (though with a changing climate it seems earlier every year) clumps of delicate snowdrops appear on the verges and in woodland clearings. They are followed by the first shoots of the bare trees and a subtle greening of the woods. Blackthorn is the hedgerow plant to blossom first, in masses of exquisite ice-white flowers. Soon after, it's the turn of hawthorn to flower in white and pink clouds, and the first cow parsley sparkles white in the verges. Bluebells cover the ground of broad-leafed woods in shimmering iridescence. Spring has truly sprung and early summer is not far away. On a rare few lost lanes, most often where it's a little damp, is wild garlic. I often smell it before I see it, but the starry white flowers and long, glossy, deep green leaves are easily spotted. It's one of the tastiest wild plants and has plenty of uses: in place of basil in a pasta, or like spinach in an omelette or a pie.

In the first week of the Tour de France, the world's greatest bicycle race, there are always always a few shots of the peloton as it speeds by a gigantic field of sunflowers, each tilting its cheery round face towards the riders. Most of Britain lacks the climate for such displays, but our wild equivalent of the sunflower must surely be the oxeye daisy. It can be found on roadsides in huge numbers and makes for an equally colourful, uplifting sight. Scarlet poppies appear in clusters on verges and occasionally in drifts across fields of wheat and barley. They share the roadside with hundreds of other types of wild flowers. Creamy meadowsweet, purple spires of foxgloves and pale blue puffs of scabious floating on long stems are are just three of the easiest to spot, but there are many, many more. Such is the habitat value of these verges that the charity Plantlife has a campaign to encourage local councils to look after them better, which mostly means letting them grow and set seed, only cutting them at certain times of the year.

As high summer passes into August and September, the fresh green fades to a duller hue, the swallows and swifts gather for their long flights to Africa, and the fields are emptied of their crops. Blackberries fill the hedgerows, offering themselves to passing cyclists as a natural energy food with an unsurpassed taste when eaten straight from the hedge. Soon the temperature falls, the days shorten, and it's easy to feel a little down at the thought of the long winter ahead. But on some autumn days the skies miraculously brighten and clear, and a crisp autumn day is one of the most precious of the year. Under a cloudless blue sky are autumn leaves in countless shades of red and gold; it's a psychedelic display and every bit the equal of the firework spectaculars of Bonfire Night.

Eventually deep winter takes its grip and the countryside turns monochrome, with trees revealing their essential forms in the low beams of the weak winter sun. On really cold days, the fields are frost-dusted and any seed-heads still standing are encrusted with glittering ice. It looks as though nothing is growing, but the first green blades of winter-sown wheat are already emerging from the soil, the very first suggestion of the real spring that's still a month or more away.

When we pay attention to our surroundings, going for a bike ride is so much more than turning the pedals and counting the miles. It's an inspiration that can dispel the blackest mood, it's

a real education in geography and geology, history and culture, it's an easy and inexpensive way of spending carefree time with friends and family, it's a radical demonstration of independence and self-sufficiency – taken all together, it's a new way of seeing the world that begins right on our doorsteps. Enjoy the ride!

FURTHER READING

W. G. HOSKINS: *The Making Of the English Landscape* 1955, new edition 2005. A classic, pioneering work that combines the lyrical and academic.

FRANCIS PRYOR: *The Making of the British Landscape* 2010. A modern take on Hoskins' study, drawing on the latest methods of archaeology and ecology.

OLIVER RACKHAM: *Trees and Woodland in the British Landscape* 1976, revised 1990. There is no greater expert on British woods.

RICHARD MABEY: *Flora Britannica* 1996. Landmark guide to the plants of the British Isles and the history and folklore that surrounds them.

RICHARD MABEY: *The Unofficial Countryside* 1973, new edition 2010. A left-field look at the often neglected countryside that's all around us.

CLIVE ASLET: *Villages of Britain* 2010. Fascinating insight into rural life through the ages, seen through the stories of 500 villages.

SIMON JENKINS: *England's Thousand Best Churches* 1999. A guidebook to the great dispersed museum of art, craft and architecture that is housed in England's churches.

SUE CLIFFORD AND ANGELA KING: *England in Particular* 2006. An informative alphabetical compendium of the commonplace, the local and the distinctive.

BEST FOR

WILD CAMPING

—

Nights in a tent in the back garden were a highlight of my childhood summers. It was just a few steps from the back door of our London terraced house, but for a nine-year-old with a fertile imagination camping offered a whole new world of adventure. The smell of the cool night air, the strange sounds of nocturnal birds and animals, the mysterious dew that soaked everything, the thrill of a 'midnight feast' and chatting with friends late into the night, far away from adult ears. On clear nights, there was the magic of the moon and stars.

In the years that followed I have travelled further afield, more often than not by bicycle, wild camping along the way. The realities of work and home life now conspire to make it more difficult to disappear on long-distance adventures, but my desire for the pleasures of sleeping under the stars remains undiminished. That is why, over the past ten years, I've taken to going for short, overnight bicycle trips: leaving after work and returning the next morning having camped out somewhere quiet and beautiful.

Many of the routes in this book could be used as the basis for a short overnight trip with a small tent or bivvy bag. They're best on a long summer evening when there's plenty of time to ride for a few hours, find a remote and beautiful spot and enjoy a simple camp dinner before settling down to a night under the stars, safe in the knowledge that you'll be returning to real life the next morning. There's no need for all the stressful preparation and packing for a longer trip. If you forget something, it's no big deal. The worst that can happen is a bad night's sleep.

Rather than cook an elaborate camp dinner, I tend to fill a Thermos flask with something hot and hearty, and perhaps cook up some couscous on a lightweight camping stove; packing a loaf of bread means the stove can be left behind altogether. Perhaps the biggest challenge on an overnight trip is carrying enough water. Two to three litres per person allows for drinking plenty while riding, some for cooking in the evening and enough for tea or coffee in the morning. I leave the washing up until I get home, to save water and bother, keeping dirty utensils in a plastic bag. If you do run dry, most pubs will be happy to refill your bottles.

A recent trip to the North Downs must count as among my most memorable. It was only about an hour's ride from central London and as we ate our dinner we watched the stars appear twinkling in a surprisingly dark sky. There's nothing more relaxing than sitting at a camp, well fed, relaxing and chatting by candlelight, feeling the cool night breeze and watching the night sky, the cares of the city left far behind. The orange glow of London was hidden by a dark hill to the north, and all we heard were the hoots of tawny owls in the wood above us and the bleating of sheep in the valley below. It was hard to believe we were still well within the ring of the M25.

DO IT YOURSELF

Finding a good place for an overnight camping trip is easier with a little preparation. It's worth looking at the Ordnance Survey's 1:25,000 Explorer maps to get an idea of promising locations. The best spots are out of sight of any dwellings, on open land, preferably with access by a bridleway or footpath. It can help to take a little time on a day ride to scout out a potential camping spot and make a note of the location for a future trip.

If you are camping near to a footpath or bridleway, or on the outskirts of a town or village, it's prudent to set up a little way away, out of sight of early morning dog-walkers. A tent adds weight and can make you more conspicuous, but it gives a sense of security and more protection from the elements and flying insects. Sleeping in a hammock or under a tarp is an interesting alternative to a tent or a bivvy bag. It comes down to a matter of taste: some find hammocks uncomfortable, others dislike the confinement of a tent.

With the exception of open access areas of the South Downs National Park, wild camping is not legal in southern England. Either ask for permission from the landowner or take the pragmatic view that as long as you're unseen and leave no evidence of ever having been there, the landowner is unlikely ever to know, or to care, that you've spent the night. If it's farmland, be sure not to disturb any livestock or trample any crops. Don't light fires without permission, and leave the site in a better state than you found it by collecting any litter left by other visitors.

The following rides in this book are particularly well suited for adapting into a wild camping trip.

A QUINTESSENCE OF ENGLAND (RIDE No. 8)

It's a bit of a grunt up the hill from the southern edge of this route, but once up on the ridge of the South Downs there are plenty of places to unfurl a sleeping bag and enjoy the view.

RIVER TO RIDGEWAY (RIDE No. 18)

The Ridgeway at the western edge of this route is a wild and dramatic landscape with views into the vale of White Horse and Didcot power station.

SURREY HILLS LEGBUSTER (RIDE No. 11)

Much of the land is owned by the National Trust, which has bylaws against wild camping, but the North Downs is full of secluded places where an overnight bivvy will go entirely undetected.

WINCHESTER WINTER WARMER (RIDE No. 14)

The South Downs is a national park and there's plenty of open land to find a good spot up high above the Meon Valley. Exercise caution if there are livestock around.

THE WILD WEALD (RIDE No. 7)

There is no shortage of places to disappear into the woods high up in the Ashdown Forest, and some fine views of the surrounding countryside.

HIDDEN HERTFORDSHIRE (RIDE No. 21)

The ancient Icknield Way crosses the western end of this ride, and there are many good spots for an overnight camp or bivvy, either in the woods or out in the open.

Always ask permission before lighting fires

BEST FOR

WEEKENDS AWAY

—

All of the rides in this book can be done in a day, but the longer ones or those that are a little further afield make sense as a weekend trip with an overnight stay. Britain's tourism infrastructure has improved over recent years with the revival in local and regional gastronomy, the refurbishment of tired hotels and a dawning realisation that we don't have to get on a plane for a fantastic holiday.

There is a wide range of places to stay, from tiny get-back-to-nature campsites, through camping barns, youth hostels and holiday cottages to plush B&Bs and exquisite boutique hotels. The internet makes finding a good place a thousand times easier.

The Fox Inn, Ride No. 19

THE FIFTH CONTINENT (RIDE No. 4)

The small, lively maritime town of Rye makes for an excellent weekend destination, and this ride fits the bill perfectly. The new high-speed train to Ashford makes light work of the journey to deepest Kent. An alternative to Rye is the pretty hillside village of Winchelsea, something of an artists' colony in Victorian and Edwardian times.

ESCAPE TO COOKHAM ISLAND (RIDE No. 16)

The Environment Agency maintains a handful of tiny campsites on its river locks and Cookham is among the best. It's on the tip of a little island in the Thames, a short ride from the village of Cookham, where the artist Stanley Spencer lived and worked. This part of the Thames Valley can feel crowded at times, but even in the height of summer Cookham Lock is a car-free oasis of calm.

AROUND THE WIGHT (RIDE No. 15)

Riding around the Wight in a single day leaves little time to stop and take in the spectacular views, explore the beaches, enjoy a lazy pub lunch or indulge in a calorie-laden cream tea. Making it a weekend away or even a three-day trip gives plenty of time to get to know England's biggest island, a scenic secret that hides in plain sight on the south coast.

SUN, SEA & SUFFOLK (RIDE No. 26)

Nobody regrets tarrying a while on the Suffolk coast. The county is among the sunniest in Britain and there's plenty to explore, from the huge nature reserve at Minsmere to medieval churches and ruined abbeys. Then there's the seaside: from upmarket Southwold to arty Aldeburgh and sleepy Walberswick. Stay at the Ship Inn at Dunwich or camp out in a tipi, yurt or gypsy caravan at Alde Garden, a quirky countryside hideaway.

CRAB & WINKLE (RIDE No. 5)

Bike-friendly Nethergong Nurseries, on the edge of the Isle of Thanet and just a few miles from Canterbury, could just be Britain's perfect campsite. It's very spacious with plenty of trees for shade, several

large lakes and ponds and the bonus of home-grown fruit and veg. There's wild swimming in the River Stour, the seaside only a few miles away, a burgeoning cultural renaissance in Margate and oysters and art a-plenty at Whitstable.

WAVENEY WEEKENDER (RIDE No. 27)

The Waveney is a jewel-like river that winds a short course along the border between Suffolk and Norfolk. A fast train to Diss makes the valley accessible for a wonderful weekend away. The cycling is extremely gentle and on very quiet lanes, with plenty of places to stop for a river dip, a picnic or a pub lunch or a nose around one of Suffolk's lovely and historic village churches.

A COTSWOLD GETAWAY (RIDE No. 19)

This ride is perfectly suited for a weekend trip, with an overnight stay in handsome Stow-on-the-Wold or any of the picture-perfect villages of this part of the eastern Cotswolds. There's plenty of choice, from traditional hotels and country inns to small, family-run B&Bs and tiny campsites.

Anyone looking to really splash out and spend a night in style will face the onerous task of choosing between Lower Slaughter Manor and the Michelin-starred Lords of the Manor a little further along the lane in Upper Slaughter.

BEST FOR
GOURMETS

Eating delicious food is one of the rewards of cycle touring. A day in the saddle brings with it a healthy appetite, and all the exercise gives a green light to tasty temptations that might trouble the more calorie-conscious, whether it's morning coffee and pastries, cream teas on a village green, fish and chips on the beach, a hefty pub lunch in the sunshine or a long, luxurious picnic of local delicacies under the shade of a spreading tree.

Britain is in grip of a local food revolution that is encouraging regional distinctiveness, reviving local specialities and celebrating small-scale local production. Nobody benefits more than the touring cyclist, who is free stop off to enjoy all the variety on offer. Cycling gives us a better sense of what the French call *terroir*: the unique combination of climate, soil, topography and tradition that is the secret of the very best local foods.

THE OYSTER RUN (RIDE No. 24)

The Romans elevated the Colchester Native oyster to the status of national treasure. It's prized by connoisseurs and served in the world's best restaurants, but there's nowhere better to eat a dozen than at the rough and ready Company Shed down by the boatyards of West Mersea. After lunch, ride through the Essex fruit orchards and stop in Tiptree for scones and tea at the Wilkin & Sons jam factory.

CRAB & WINKLE (RIDE No. 5)

Whitstable is famous for its oysters (and its cockles and mussels, winkles and whelks) but there's much more than molluscs in this pretty, artsy seaside town. Seafood of every kind is on offer, from the cheap and cheerful stalls around the harbour to high class joints like Wheeler's and the Whitstable Oyster Company.

EVERYTHING STOPS FOR TEA (RIDE No. 13)

Sunday afternoon teas on the green in the pretty village of Brockham during the summer (late April to October) set a high standard for villages across the country to aspire to. Delicious homemade cakes on offer, with all proceeds going to local good causes.

AROUND THE WIGHT (RIDE No. 15)

Bembridge is renowned for its crabs and lobsters. Its shallow bay and clean water make for smaller specimens, prized for their sweetness.

The sunny climes of the Isle of Wight are also good growing conditions for many Mediterranean vegetables, and the island holds an annual garlic festival.

SUN, SEA & SUFFOLK (RIDE No. 26)

East Anglia is pig country, and Emmett's in Peasenhall have been curing bacon and ham since 1820. Their deli-café is a foodie paradise. Suffolk lanes are dotted with fruit and vegetable stands where home gardeners put their surplus production out for sale, often with fantastic free-range eggs on offer as well.

Whitstable, Ride No. 5

BEST FOR
UPS AND DOWNS

—

Freewheeling down a long hill is one of the great pleasures of life, good times distilled into a handful of seconds. A steeper slope and faster speed add a shot of adrenalin to the pleasurable cocktail. Riding downhill is a miracle of weightless, noiseless, effortless travel and the closest most of us come to experiencing the thrill of flying without actually donning a parachute and jumping out of an aeroplane.

But there is a catch: what goes down must also go up. And riding a bicycle uphill is, at the very least, an acquired taste. On the flat the bicycle is a miracle machine, a magic carpet that multiplies a modest effort into near effortless speed. On a climb, the tables are turned. It is the bicycle that makes demands of the rider. Suddenly the miracle machine is a dead-weight burden to bear.

Yet there are times when the climb is an experience of sublime exultation and perfectly measured effort. Every rhythm, from beating heart to heaving lungs to pumping legs and spinning pedals, comes together in a single symphony of ascent. Be it in a state of grace or of grim determination, the most immediate reward of a climbing a hill is the same: it's over. The relief is dramatic and instantaneous. The all-consuming struggle fades quickly into memory. There's time to pause, take in the view, and get ready for the real fun, the descent.

THE WILD WEALD (RIDE No. 7)

The crinkly, wooded hills of the Weald are a veritable roller-coaster: when the road is not going up, it's going down. This ride takes in Kidds Hill, tellingly known as 'The Wall', a favourite hill climb among local cyclists.

Box Hill, Ride No. 11

Military Road, Ride No. 15

SURREY HILLS LEGBUSTER (RIDE No. 11)

The ultimate test: as much climbing as the most famous of Alpine cols, with views to match on fine days. Better tea shops and pubs than anywhere in the Pyrenees.

CHILTERN RENDEZVOUS (RIDE No. 20)

Ivinghoe Beacon is the most prominent summit of the Chilterns and a long, hard grind on a bicycle. It lacks the brutality to be found of the hills south of London, but from the top you can see for miles and miles.

AROUND THE WIGHT (RIDE No. 15)

The southern coast road of the Wight is an up-down-up-again affair, with two eye-watering descents: from St Catherine's Hill through Blackgang to Chale, and from the top of the Afton Down into Freshwater Bay.

WINCHESTER WINTER WARMER (RIDE No. 14)

The western end of the South Downs is hill country, and the hard work of the climbs is paid back in full with a long, straight and fast descent into Winchester.

A THAMES MEANDER (RIDE No. 17)

From high-altitude Stoke Row to the Thames at Wallingford is one of the best long descents in southern England, much of it on classic lost lanes. Two outstanding pubs *en route* are well placed to help wring out every last ounce of pleasure.

HOUSES & HILLS (RIDE No. 2)

Kentish hills are the toughest in southern England, and this ride takes in the famous Yorks Hill, the stage for the world's oldest bicycle race. Fortunately it goes down it, though the long climb up past Ightham Mote at the end of the day is a real test.

BEST FOR

HISTORY

—

In the countryside you can see landscape and history collide. Geology, climate and nature play the leading roles, but humans have wrought profound changes, from cutting down whole forests to building towns, taming rivers and constructing canals, roads and railways. Wars, plagues, floods, political change and religious upheaval have all left their marks in the landscape.

Ripley, Ride No. 12

All of this shaped the lives of the multitudes of ordinary folk who left no written record of their own. The texture of their lives can best be felt by seeing for oneself the places where our forebears lived and loved, worked and worshipped.

WINCHESTER WINTER WARMER (RIDE No. 14)

Winchester is thought to have been an important Iron Age settlement and was later the home of Alfred the Great, the king of Wessex who defended England against Viking invaders. The Normans moved the capital to London, but built Winchester a fine cathedral. The remote Meon Valley boasts lovely churches, both Saxon and Norman.

GARDEN CITY (RIDE No. 29)

There are few cities that are a match for London, and a tour around the city's parks and open spaces offers plenty of interest for the historian, from cathedrals and museums to palaces and old pubs. The only constant is change, as the city continues to be rebuilt and reshaped.

THE FIFTH CONTINENT (RIDE No. 4)

Time and tide have shaped the Romney Marsh and Dungeness, but so too has mankind, converting a disease-ridden swamp into valuable land for grazing sheep and growing crops, not to mention building a nuclear power station and offshore wind farms. Medieval churches still rise above the flat landscape as a reminder of past days in this strange corner of Kent.

VALLEY OF VISION (RIDE No. 1)

A Roman villa, a Norman castle, an Elizabethan manor, a Victorian mill town and a Battle of Britain museum offer up a crash course in two thousand years of English history in a single day.

THE RIPLEY ROAD (RIDE No. 12)

The first generations of London cyclists favoured the Ripley Road and, while little of their old route down remains, the A3 bypass has returned the village some of its former charm. Cycle jumbles in the village hall offer more concrete opportunities to take home a piece of bicycling history.

THE LONELIEST LANDSCAPE (RIDE No. 6)

The Hoo peninsula renders the majesty of the Thames Estuary in all its haunting, eerie glory. It's a landscape that inspired Dickens and Conrad, and there's plenty of history to be discovered beneath its big skies.

St Mary in the Marsh, Ride No. 4

Farningham, Ride No. 1

Newark Priory, Ride No. 12

All Saints, East Meon, Ride No. 14

BEST FOR

VILLAGE LIFE

———

'To the man or woman who is desirous of finding the best in this country I commend the English village' wrote the poet Edmund Blunden shortly after the second world war. Even today, it is villages that so often define the character of the English countryside: the church, the green, the pub, the village shop, the red phone box. A fortunate few have retained one of each of these and perhaps more: a well, a duck pond or a windmill. They are the trappings of a certain romantic view of the immutable English village: fixed in time, never changing, the steady constant amid the perpetual motion of urban life.

But it's a mythical view. Villages do change with the times, in spite of stringent planning laws and rampant NIMBYism. Some grow, others shrink, an unfortunate few disappear altogether. Not so long ago, rural life was more often characterised by poverty and deprivation, and people sought better lives in the cities. In the past few decades, much of the countryside has become altogether more affluent, as people fulfil a dream of comfortable country living while holding down lucrative jobs elsewhere, or working remotely thanks to the internet. Villages no longer support a butcher, a baker and a candlestick maker; shopping is fetched by car. To the car and the internet must be added a third profound force of change: farming. Agriculture may still dominate the landscape but mechanisation means it now employs hardly anybody.

In some villages the old ways die hard, and something of a renaissance can be detected, celebrating local distinctiveness, folk traditions and a spirit of cooperation. Blunden's commendation still holds true, and he might have added that bicycles are not just best way to discover the charms of the English village, they positively enhance the village scene.

A QUINTESSENCE OF ENGLAND (RIDE No. 8)

This quiet corner of West Sussex has more than a few lovely villages but two stand out. Lurgashall, whose wide expanse of village green is home to perhaps the most idyllic cricket pitch in the country, and Lodsworth, whose residents are rightly proud of their fabulous and cooperatively run village shop.

JOY OF ESSEX (RIDE No. 25)

A renowned centre of Morris dancing, Thaxted boasts fine half-timbered buildings, an impressively spired church and a sturdy windmill. But for looks alone, picture-perfect Finchingfield must be the jewel in the crown in this most scenic corner of northern Essex.

A THAMES MEANDER (RIDE No. 17)

A sweep of Thames villages, from sleepy Sonning, 'the most fairy-like little nook of the whole river', according to Jerome K. Jerome in *Three Men In a Boat*, to the wealthy Upper and Lower Shiplakes and last, over the hill, Brightwell-cum-Sotwell, the heart-breakingly beautiful marriage of two perfect Oxfordshire villages.

VALLEY OF VISION (RIDE No. 1)

When it comes to villages, the Darent valley has an embarrassment of riches. Architecturally, Farningham is the most grand, and its annual village fête is everything such an event should be, while the stream running down the main street at Eynsford is perfect for summer paddling. Pretty Shoreham retains its ramshackle charm, nowhere more so than in its colourful allotments and annual duck race.

Shoreham, Ride No. 1

Lodsworth, Larder Ride No. 8

Sonning Lock, Ride No. 17

BEST FOR

WILD SWIMMING

—

Several of the world's top professional bike racing teams have installed ultra-cold immersion tanks on board their team buses, on the basis that a dip in cold water rejuvenates tired legs. The touring cyclist can dispense with such gadgetry and simply take a plunge in the sea or in a river, lake or waterfall. On a hot summer's day a wild swim is an unsurpassable delight. People who have only ever swum in the sanitised clear waters of chlorinated pools might feel a little hesitant about sharing the water with ducks, swans and fish, or touching toes with the mildly unsettling reedy strands that grow up through the murky ooze below. As a society we've lost touch with the tradition of outdoor swimming in natural surroundings, but it's remarkable how many secluded swimming holes and empty beaches there are out there just waiting to be found.

A few safety considerations include making sure that you're not trespassing on private land, being alert to the strength of the tide or the flow of the river and checking the depth of the water before diving or jumping in. For a whole new world of wild swimming, read Roger Deakin's classic *Waterlog* and Daniel Start's superb guidebooks *Wild Swimming* and *Hidden Beaches*.

WAVENEY WEEKENDER (RIDE No. 27)

The favourite river of Roger Deakin, the godfather of wild swimming, the Waveney is a paradise of sweet waters in the lush rolling landscape of the Suffolk-Norfolk border.

A THAMES MEANDER (RIDE No. 17)

Plenty of swimming spots on the Thames between Sonning and Henley, easily accessible by bicycle along the Thames Path.

River Thames, Ride No. 17

AROUND THE WIGHT (RIDE No. 15)

On a circumnavigation of southern England's scenic Isle of Wight the sea is never far away, from the sweeping sandy beaches of Compton Bay to the steep pebble shore and spectacular cliffs at Freshwater Bay.

TURF & SURF (RIDE No. 9)

West Wittering is a spectacular, long sandy beach for swimming and surfing. Take care with the high tide at Bosham Harbour, or your swim may be of the involuntary variety.

EMPTY ESSEX (RIDE No. 23)

White sands, blue waters, big skies. The swimming spots on the north-east tip of the Dengie Peninsula are little-known gems.

CRAB & WINKLE (RIDE No. 5)

A sea swim at Whitstable or Herne Bay in the morning, and another in the freshwater of the River Stour in the afternoon. What more could the wild-swimming cyclist wish for?

River Waveney, Ride No. 27

West Wittering, Ride No. 9

Isle of Wight, Ride No. 15

37

BEST FOR
FAMILIES

For new cyclists and younger children, sharing even quiet country lanes with motor traffic can be unnerving, but that's no reason not to head out for a few hours on two wheels. Fortunately, thanks to the dogged work of Sustrans and enlightened public bodies, every year sees more miles of traffic-free cycling to enjoy. Riverside paths, canal towpaths, off-road cycle tracks and bridleways are an enjoyable, safe and confidence-building alternative to roads and lanes.

For children, exploring places is a rewarding day out. Adult learners will find even a modest journey in beautiful surroundings a pleasurable introduction to what bicycle travel can offer. Traffic-free routes also make for relaxing, stress-free rides for more experienced cyclists, though on shared paths it's important to slow down and give priority to people out walking.

WINDSOR GREAT PARK (RIDE No. 10)

There's nowhere better for children and adults to learn to ride than the wide, smooth paths of this huge park, formerly the private hunting ground of England's royalty and still owned and managed by the Crown Estate.

TURF & SURF (RIDE No. 9)

While not wholly traffic-free, this ride is on quiet lanes and can be further adapted to maximise the amount of gentle, flat, off-road riding. Children will love the beach at West Wittering, and taking your bike on the ferry to Bosham reveals all its adaptable, go-anywhere glory to new cyclists.

GARDEN CITY (RIDE No. 29)

Not all of this ride is off-road, but the section in the Royal Parks makes for a brilliant traffic-free day out in the centre of London. There are plenty of sights to see, and the whole journey through the Royal Parks from Buckingham Palace to Kensington Palace can be made on entirely off-road cycle paths. It's best on Sundays, when The Mall and Constitution Hill are closed to motor traffic, offering even more space for walkers, skaters and cyclists.

WIMBLEDON TO WEYBRIDGE (RIDE No. 30)

Perhaps this route is too long for younger children to ride in a single day, but it links together many scenic and motor-free stretches of south-west London that are perfect places for a family ride. The traffic-free circular route around Richmond Park is ideal for beginner riders, and good-quality hire bikes are available there, so lack of your own machine is no reason not to give it a go.

Richmond Park, Ride No. 30

BEST FOR

PUBS

——

The pub, like the church and the green, is a focal point that helps define the English village. Yet across the country, pubs are closing at an alarming rate. Many of those that remain have become quasi-restaurants offering upmarket dining or, at the other end of the scale, rural sports bars with giant television screens and Saturday night karaoke.

Pubs date back to Anglo-Saxon times, when people opened their homes as alehouses, hence the term 'public house'. The modern system of landlords licensed by local magistrates dates back to 1552, and was the result of concerns about drunkenness and public order. But, as George Orwell observed, people don't go to pubs to get drunk. They go for a drink or two, certainly, but they mostly go to enjoy good company in a convivial atmosphere.

Despite the closures, the pub is fighting back. Microbreweries are breathing new life into the art of beer-making and the tireless Campaign for Real Ale (CAMRA) not only leads the crusade for authentic tipples but also maintains a fantastic directory of historic pub interiors.

RIVER TO RIDGEWAY (RIDE No. 18)

People travel a long way for a pint and a crusty roll at the Bell, either inside its wooden interior or in its sunny garden. As village pubs go, it's as good as it gets.

FARMLAND FANTASTIC (RIDE No. 22)

Only ten pubs in Britain have no bar or serving hatch, and the Cock is one of them, a cosy red-tiled warren of five tiny rooms centred around a sunken tap room.

WINCHESTER WINTER WARMER (RIDE No. 14)

A string of pubs tempt you along on the ride up the Itchen, including one serving beer from the local Flowerpots brewery. At the end of the ride waits the Black Boy, a brilliantly eccentric Winchester institution.

THE FIFTH CONTINENT (RIDE No. 4)

In the same family for nearly a century, the Red Lion at Snargate is a portal to another era. Electricity was installed only reluctantly and is confined to a single bulb in each of the small, snug rooms.

BETWEEN DOWNS & WEALD (RIDE No. 3)

As a home-counties country pub, the Spotted Dog is hard to beat. It has a cosy, low-ceilinged interior and a back terrace with gorgeous views over the forests of the Weald towards Penshurst Place.

A THAMES MEANDER (RIDE No. 17)

Two excellent pubs in close succession are a reward for the long climb up from Henley to Stoke Row. The Black Horse at Checkendon has been in the same family for a century, and the King William IV at Hailey has a fabulous sunset terrace overlooking the Thames valley as far as the Ridgeway.

SUN, SEA & SUFFOLK (RIDE No. 26)

Easy riding on quiet, very gently rolling countryside and a sprinkling of good village pubs, many serving local beer from the Adnams brewery in Southwold.

The Bell Inn, Aldworth, Ride No. 18

The Star Inn, Wenhaston, Ride No. 26

Kentish hops, Ride No. 3

KENT

VALLEY OF VISION

Just twenty miles from central London, the Darent valley is still an arcadian Kentish landscape of orchards, hop fields and unspoilt villages.

———

In the 1820s a handful of young British artists rejected a London art scene dominated by stuffy society portraiture, and formed a breakaway group that sought to get back to nature. Although barely into their twenties, they dubbed themselves 'the Ancients', an allusion to their rejection of the modern world of teeming cities and dirty factories. Their hero was the visionary poet, engraver and painter William Blake, whose mystical work had fallen out of fashion, leaving him near poverty and in failing health. The ringleader was the young painter Samuel Palmer, who had upped sticks from 'horrid smoky London' and moved to the small village of Shoreham in the Darent Valley of north-west Kent. Together, the group produced a body of work that prefigured the pre-Raphaelites and Impressionists.

Palmer and his friends went on rambles along the valley, through the cornfields and over the rounded hills, exploring ruins, walking long into the night and generally basking in their own talent and eccentricity. Palmer grew a long beard and wore a cloak down to his heels. It was a serious undertaking, but there was an innocent fun at the heart of it, and much drinking of cider. For them, the Darent valley was an arcadia; Palmer described it as his 'valley of vision'. I wanted to see whether what

had so inspired those young artists was still to be found two centuries later.

As I fairly flew down the hill from Swanley, the wind filling my eyes with tears, I wondered if the Ancients, who were firm opponents of the 'machine age' would have made an exception for bicycles had they been invented in the 1820s. The industrial revolution transformed the first villages I came to into sizeable mill towns, harnessing the power of the river to feed a booming Victorian economy. South Darenth had a flour mill powered initially by water and later by coal, while Horton Kirby's vast paper mill employed as many as 400 people. It too had a flour mill, which was later repurposed to make shoelaces and electrical cables. Some light industry remains, but most of the buildings fell into dereliction and have recently been converted into housing.

A towering railway viaduct separates the two villages and as I rolled beneath its arches I met a carriage pulled by pair of dray horses with glossy coats and billowing blonde manes. Soon after, I found that a summer fête was in full swing on the playing fields by the river. There was a Punch and Judy stand, a colourful troupe of Morris dancers dressed in dark, voodoo-like costumes, a mobile belfry offering bell-ringing workshops and trestle tables laden with cakes and scones for tea. If I was

---

START & FINISH: Swanley, Kent • DISTANCE: 22 miles/36km • TOTAL ASCENT: 437m • TERRAIN: Mostly quiet lanes; a brief section of off-road track that could be muddy after heavy rain. Moderate.

Shoreham

Shoreham

Farningham

riding in search of a pastoral arcadia, all the signs were looking good.

The name Darent (or Darenth, as it is found in the village name) is thought to derive from the ancient British *Deorwente*, Latinised by the Romans to *Deruentio*, meaning 'oak river'. In Edmund Spenser's poem *The Faerie Queen*, praise for the tributaries of the Thames singles out 'the still Darent, in whose waters clean / Ten thousand fishes play, and deck her pleasant stream'. Kingfishers and dragonflies are the iridescent star turns in the large cast of wildlife that enjoys the tumbling waters today.

Here the river cuts a steep valley through the North Downs, and the lanes climb gently towards Farningham. The village boasts some very grand buildings, a large waterside pub and a curious folly bridge, or 'cattle screen' to prevent cows wandering up the shallow river, depending on who you ask. On the road out of Farningham, bright red poppies peppered the fields on the other side of the valley, and shortly after I came to a halt by a small memorial stone to Flight Lieutenant James Paterson from the Royal New Zealand Air Force, who died here in 1940, when his Spitfire was shot down during the Battle of Britain. He was just 20 and a long way from home.

I crossed the river at Eynsford, by the bridge and not the ford (which would have been fun to watch), to take a look at the ruins of Eynsford Castle. Despite falling into disrepair way back in the 14th century and being used for a time by local landowners as dog kennels, it is said to be one of the most complete Norman castles in England, and is now maintained by English Heritage and free to enter. Some very tall walls remain, enormous structures in flint and chalk, and the kids running around were having no trouble imagining they were medieval soldiers, some storming the dried-up moat while others repelled their attacks from the battlements.

I slipped even farther back in time as I continued up the valley along Lullingstone Lane, past the remains of a Roman villa discovered in the 1940s and now also run by English Heritage (£). It boasts some impressive mosaic floors and a pagan shrine apparently devoted to local water deities, with a wall painting of three water nymphs. The Ancients were greatly inspired by Virgil's pastoral poetry and would have found the place captivating. It's a shame it was hidden beneath their feet.

The lane peters out in front of Lullingstone Castle, a large manor house that can be seen through a towering red brick Tudor gateway. The estate is home to the idisyncratic World Garden of Plants (£), created by Tom Hart Dyke, the current heir to the estate. At the age of 24, while on a plant-hunting expedition, Tom found himself at the wrong end of an AK-47 automatic rifle, taken hostage in the Colombian jungle. He spent what he thought would

be his final days designing his dream garden; freed after being held captive for nine months, he came home and set about turning his dream into reality. The estate has other claims to fame: this is where the rules of lawn tennis were first codified, and where the silk used in Queen Elizabeth II's coronation robes and wedding dress was produced.

Beyond Lullingstone, the track becomes a footpath through the woods along the edge of a lake. This is not a cycle path, and though it is quite rideable and many people do ride through here, it may be polite and prudent to walk, particularly if there are other people enjoying a walk in the woods.

I emerged from the woodland into the visitor centre and café of Lullingstone Country Park, a public park with walks and bike routes over its 460 acres of woodlands, heath and meadows, where wildflowers and orchids abound in late spring and early summer. The natural feel of the place is a little diminished by the two golf courses that spread over the land, but there's more than enough space to find a secluded picnic spot with a fine view without risk of being thwacked in the head by a flying golf ball.

Leaving the park behind me I rode into the late-afternoon glow of what appeared to be a corner of the south of France relocated to north-west Kent: the huge, purple lavender fields of Castle Farm. The best time to visit here is late July, just before the crop is harvested. The farm runs organised tours (£) but the greatest pleasure is really to be found in the fields, marvelling at the colour and the powerful scent, listening to the buzzing of bees in the hazy summer sunshine. At this moment it was hard to believe centre of the biggest city in Europe was less than 20 miles away.

Finally, my journey up the Darent had brought me to Shoreham, the home of Samuel Palmer and his band of Ancients. It retains a cheerful, slightly dishevelled village feel and an artistic reputation. Every May, the residents hold what must be the country's most colourful and anarchic river race for plastic ducks of all designs and sizes. I passed by the allotments, where results of the recent judging were pinned to the noticeboard, and then a series of delicious cottage gardens erupting with climbing flowers.

At Shoreham there was a choice to be made: I could either retrace my tracks back to Eynsford or take in an extra loop on the eastern side of the valley, up the steep hill towards the crest of the Downs. There was still plenty of light in the sky, so I pressed on. The ride this far had been flat and easy going, and I didn't mind the tough grind up

Eynsford

Railway bridge near Eynsford

the hill, along a narrow wooded lane. The views from the top were worth the 150 metres of vertical ascent. Once out of the trees, the lane along the ridge has fine views, first to the east and then north, all the way to the Thames at Dartford.

From here I began the second eye-watering descent of the day back through Eynsford before a final, leg-busting climb up Crockenhill Lane. A hundred years ago the land around here produced one of the country's biggest crops of peppermint. It must have smelled amazing.

At the top of the hill I took one look back at Palmer's 'perfumed and enchanted twilight' before I crossing back over the M25. Behind me I left the landscape described by the painter Edward Calvert, Palmer's friend and fellow Ancient, as 'a valley so hidden, that it looked as if the devil had not found it out'. Nearly two centuries later, it feels as though the devil is still none the wiser.

Download route info at thebikeshow.net/01VV

PUBS & PIT STOPS

THE LION Farningham DA4 0DP (01322 860621) Large, red brick pub in a superb location, right by the river.

THE CHEQUERS Farningham DA4 0DT (01322 865 222) Proper old-fashioned village pub with a good selection of ales and unpretentious food.

HONEY POT Shoreham TN14 7TD (01959 524 070) Tiny teashop popular with cyclists and walkers, recently named the best in England by a countryside magazine.

THE TWO BREWERS 30 High Street, Shoreham TN14 7TD (01959 522800) Recently refurbished with an airy look and specialising in home-cooked food.

SHOREHAM AIRCRAFT MUSEUM Shoreham TN14 7TB (01959 524416) Classic English tea room and garden at the rear of a museum dedicated to the Battle of Britain.

THE FOX & HOUNDS Romney Street TN15 6XR (01959 525428) At the top of a big hill, but worth the climb.

No.2

HOUSES & HILLS

Kent offers a thrilling ride down one of cycling's most historic hills
and a chance to admire some of the most beautiful stately homes in the land
— and who knows, maybe to buy one

———

Sevenoaks lies in the heart of the affluent Kent commuter belt and on a fast train just over half an hour from the centre of London. And yet within just a few minutes of riding east out of town I was immersed in a network of narrow lanes so deserted that there was sometimes a strip of grass growing along the middle. The towering canopies of beech trees make these lanes atmospheric places to ride, as the dappled light filters onto the road and mists hang in the air in the early morning.

I was heading for Yorks Hill, the course of the oldest continuously run bike race in the world. The Catford Cycling Club held its first hill climb here in 1887, and although the bikes of today are a fair bit lighter than they must have been back then, it's still much as it was: nasty, brutish and short, at less than a mile but with ramps up to 25% in places. It makes for a brilliant spectator sport, as the 150 or so riders set off at one-minute intervals with the crowd at the top, three or four deep, enthusiastically cheering every competitor to push on through the pain barrier. Mercifully, I was riding down Yorks Hill and not up it. It was a damp morning and my brakes squealed like a swine as I held tightly onto the levers to keep from accelerating out of control. After heavy rain the narrow and

pot-holed lane can be as dangerous to ride down as it is demanding to ride up.

From the bottom it was a gently undulating ride past the nature reserve at Bough Beech Reservoir, a top spot for bird-watching, and on through Chiddingstone, a picture-perfect collection of half-timbered buildings, a village store dating back to 1593, a cosy pub and tea rooms. The village (which I also visited on a route further west, *see* Ride No. 3), has been used as a classic English location for films from *A Room with a View* to *The Wind in the Willows*.

A few miles on, the Rock Inn made for a good lunch stop. It's named for the eerie sandstone outcrops on the nearby hills, overgrown with gnarled beech trees. As I rode on southward along the sunken lane that cuts through them, they were reminiscent of the famous ruined and tree-strangled Ta Prohm temple in the Cambodian jungle at Angkor.

From this high point it was a mostly downhill run past the grounds of Stonewall Park to Penshurst, then passing through the giant gatehouse of Penshurst Place. The medieval manor house (£) was Henry VIII's hunting lodge, after he had its previous owned beheaded. I rode along a few miles of wonderfully unexpected traffic-free cycle path through the estate

———

START & FINISH: Sevenoaks, Kent • DISTANCE: 32 miles/49km • TOTAL ASCENT: 595m
TERRAIN: Quiet lanes and one well-surfaced cycle track. Challenging.

Penshurst

with superbly scenic views in all directions. Back on the roads, I followed the valley of the upper River Medway past the Powder Mills site near Leigh, where explosives were first made for the Napoleonic Wars, through Hildenborough and towards the southern slopes of the North Downs.

I'm certain I'm not the only one who, while out cycling in the countryside, hasn't come upon a beautiful old house and fantasised about what it might be like to live there. In the 1920s a wealthy young American named Charles Henry Robinson was just such a touring cyclist. Riding along this very lane up to the Downs, he passed the Elizabethan manor house of Ightham Mote (pronounced 'item mote') and vowed that one day he would buy it. Thirty years later, he did.

The architecture critic Nikolaus Pevsner described the house as 'the most complete small medieval manor house in the country'. With some 70 rooms rambling around a central courtyard here, I can only guess how large a manor house must be for Pevsner to regard it as 'big'. When he died, Robinson left the estate to the National Trust (£) and I flashed my newly acquired membership card in exchange for a brief wander around the estate as the early autumn light began to fade. An old black bicycle stood casually in the courtyard. I took this to be as a subtle reminder of Robinson's happy times as a young cycle tourist.

The volunteer guardians were only to keen to tell me of the wild parties the house had seen when it was home to Robinson, a bon viveur by all accounts. It's always a little sad to see how these interesting old houses lose their liveliness when they pass into preserving hands. However well-intentioned, the attempts to recreate an authentic atmosphere rarely work, and the insides of the houses end up taking on the dry, dusty atmosphere of a museum.

From Ightham Mote there was still a little more gruelling uphill to endure before I reached the ridge of the North Downs, from where it was a short ride through narrow, wooded lanes around the long walls of Knole, my last landmark before looping back into Sevenoaks and the train home. This stately home is said to qualify as a 'calendar house' with at least 365 rooms, 52 staircases, 12 entrances and 7 courtyards. Even Nikolaus Pevsner would have to describe it as vast. Yet another of Henry VIII's residences, the house is now owned by the National Trust (£) but its 1,000-acre grounds are still in private hands.

Sadly, cycling is banned throughout. Maybe one day this draconian policy will be reconsidered.

The grounds of Knole include the site of the 9th-century chapel built near seven oak trees, called *Seouenaca* in Saxon, said to have given the town of Sevenoaks its name. The oaks have been replanted more than once since (and upstart sevens have been planted elsewhere), though sadly the great storm of 1987 blew six of them down. Now there are nine young trees growing in their place – but no plans to rename the town Nineoaks.

Download route info at thebikeshow.net/02HH

PUBS & PIT STOPS

BURGHESH TEA ROOM Chiddingstone TN8 7AH (01892 870326) Tea and cakes are served in this venerable shop during the week, cooked food and more space in a restaurant room are available at weekends.

TEA ROOMS Chiddingstone Castle TN8 7AD (01892 870347) The castle and gardens charge for admission, but the elegant, vintage-tinged tea rooms are open to all.

THE ROCK INN Hoath Corner TN8 7BS (01892 870296) Perfect country pub with local ales, lunchtime and evening meals, and unspoiled original features.

If the Rock is full, then consider the excellent **SPOTTED DOG**, which is just a small detour off the route (see Ride No. 3).

FIR TREE HOUSE TEAROOM Penshurst TN11 8DB (01892 870382) Exceptional tea room selling home-

made cakes and freshly baked scones. Sit out in the garden if it's sunny.

THE PLOUGH Leigh Road, Hildenborough TN11 9AJ (01732 832149) Small 16th-century inn with rooms.

THE TUCK SHOP Riding Farm Equestrian Centre, Riding Lane, Hildenborough TN11 9LN (01474 812294) No-frills cafe that's part of a riding stables. Sit on the sheltered terrace and watch the horses training in the paddock: you'll feel grateful you're riding a bicycle.

THE BUCKS HEAD Godden Green TN15 0JJ (01732 761330) Popular village pub serving Kentish beers from Shepherd Neame and reasonable food.

BIKE SHOP: The Bike Warehouse, 53-55 High Street, Sevenoaks TN13 1JF (01732 464997)

Ightham Mote

No.3

BETWEEN DOWNS & WEALD

Take a meandering ride to a country pub for lunch, add an ancient tree, a dose of
Tudor history, a wild swim and perhaps the most beautiful lost lane in Kent

---

From source to mouth, the River Eden only needs to travel 10 miles as the crow flies, but it's a river in no particular hurry, twisting and turning through the flat countryside between the Downs and the Weald for a full 25 miles. I took the slow, meandering river as my inspiration, as I was in the mood for nothing more than the gentlest of Sunday spins.

The Eden runs through some truly lovely countryside, but etymologists are confident that its name has nothing to do with the biblical Garden of Eden. In fact, it comes from Eadhelm, the local Saxon chief who built a wooden bridge over the river. Over time Eadhelmsbrigge became Eadhelm's Bridge and then Edenbridge, and the river took its name from the crossing.

Starting in Lingfield I headed north towards Crowhurst, a tiny village that is home to a giant yew tree, which was already ancient in Saxon times and, amazingly, is still growing today. Estimated to be 4,000 years old, it stands next to the church of St George. The tree may well have served as place of earlier, pre-Christian worship, and the church was built next to it as a way of adapting existing local customs.

It's a magnificent, gnarled creature, still sprouting a thick green canopy. Like many ancient yews, it's split and hollow inside, and there's even an improvised wooden door, put in by local people in the 1820s. Walking inside the tree feels a little like entering a grotto with living walls, smoothed by time and the irresistible urge felt by countless visitors to reach out and touch something so old, yet alive. I hope it continues to grow for another thousand years, and as I rode on I wondered what the Eden valley might look like then.

As long as rain keeps falling, the river Eden will continue to flow. Soon after Crowhurst the road crossed it, barely a stream at this point, cutting a narrow, steep-sided groove through the fields. Leaving the river to meander on its way, I continued my own journey up the short, steep hill to Staffhurst Wood, a small remnant of the kind of mixed broad-leafed woodland that covered much of the valley in Saxon times. In those days, the forest was not only the main source of fuel but was also used for hunting and for grazing pigs. This remaining pocket is managed primarily as a wildlife reserve by the Woodland Trust. It's worth a visit any time of the year but it's especially enchanting in spring, when the forest floor is an ethereal haze of bluebells.

It was a fast downhill run into Edenbridge and onto its long, straight high street, which traces an old Roman road from Peckham in south London to Lewes in East Sussex. The town has a

---

START & FINISH: Lingfield, Surrey • DISTANCE: 29 miles/46km • TOTAL ASCENT: 437m
TERRAIN: Quiet lanes. Moderate.

St Mary Magdalene, Cowden

history as a staging point on routes to the south coast, and there are still a few old coaching inns and buildings with precarious-looking timbered walls. In medieval times the town was a centre of the Weald's iron industry (*see* Ride No. 7), with a ready supplies of wood for making charcoal and iron ores from the clay soils. Over time, agriculture in the valley became increasingly oriented towards feeding the growing population of London. With a reliable supply of animal hides from the livestock farming and tannin from the oak forests, the town soon became known for its tanneries and leather-working companies.

Kent and Sussex have a reputation for celebrating bonfire night in grand style, and the Edenbridge Bonfire Society is one of the oldest in the country. Alongside Guy Fawkes himself, it's become a tradition to burn a contemporary celebrity hate figure. In 2012, after star cyclist Lance Armstrong was revealed as a doping cheat, the people of Edenbridge built a 30ft tall effigy of the American, stuffed him with fireworks and blew him up.

I followed the signs out of Edenbridge to Hever Castle (£), the childhood home of Anne Boleyn. Attracting the attention of Henry VIII but unwilling to settle for being just his mistress, Anne became the catalyst for the king's break from the Roman Catholic church and centuries of political and religious upheavals. Although her daughter Elizabeth would eventually become queen, Anne's failure to provide Henry with the male heir he desperately sought led to trumped up charges of adultery, incest and treason, and she was sentenced to death by burning, commuted to beheading in Henry's last gesture of kindness towards her.

As I rolled past the castle gates, I reflected that it seems a little insensitive to Anne's memory that the pub outside her home is called the King Henry VIII. Even more insultingly, perhaps, the castle passed to the king on the death of Anne's father and was given to his fourth wife, Anne of Cleves,

in a divorce settlement. It is now open to the public; the historic building is set in gardens that include an early-20th-century Italianate sculpture garden, lake walks and yew and water mazes.

Beyond Hever lies the tiny village of Chiddingstone, said to be the most perfect surviving example of a one-street Tudor village in the country. It certainly feels it: a long line of half-timbered, oak-gabled houses with red-tiled roofs, an old post office-cum-village shop and a cosy pub. The nearby Chiddingstone Castle (£), open part of the year, houses unusual Oriental and Egyptian collections, and boasts a love affair nearly as doomed as Anne and Henry's.

The countryside then opens up into wider fields, and on the road out towards Wallers Town I passed a bulky red brick building with two tremendous oast houses: round structures with conical wooden roofs, built for drying hops for beer and typical in this part of Kent. If this got me thinking about beer, fortunately it wasn't far off my route to the Spotted Dog, one of the best country pubs in Kent. The pub's rear terrace has an unsurpassed view across the valley, where the waters of the River Eden flow into the Medway. There's a good river swimming spot at the bottom of the

61

hill, in the Medway, nearby to Old Swaylands. It's reached down the track past Nashes Farm about 20 minutes off the route.

After lunch I retraced my tracks up the hill and began a 6-mile run that is probably my favourite stretch of countryside in the whole of Kent. It passes Bassetts Mill, a Tudor pearl of a house tucked into a lush green valley. Beyond Bassetts, the lovely village of Cowden is a real gem: it's less self-consciously well-preserved than Chiddingstone and all the better for it. The Fountain pub has an old enamelled 'winged wheel' sign on one of its outbuildings; as far back as the 1880s the Cyclists' Touring Club was providing these signs to pubs that catered especially well for cyclists. These days, the CTC hands out small plastic stickers that pubs and cafes can put in their windows.

The gentle ascent continues up Furnace Lane, another nod to the ironworking history of the Weald. I sometimes think of this lane as the ultimate 'lost lane': the wooded river on one side and the hillside on the other make it totally enchanting. It even has a rambling old farm house and tumbledown dovecote in dire need of repair. At the top of the lane I had just a little more climbing to do before a long, fast descent through the well-heeled village of Dormansland (home to Tom Cruise and Peter Andre, apparently) and back to Lingfield. Kent is southern England's hilliest county, but somehow I'd managed to avoid any really big hills and felt refreshed in mind and body after a perfect Sunday spin.

Download route info at thebikeshow.net/03DW

PUBS & PIT STOPS

THE ROYAL OAK Caterfield Lane, Staffhurst Wood RH8 0RR (01883 722207) Popular, old-fashioned country pub with a great views across the surrounding land.

EDENBRIDGE provided plenty of choices, including shops for picnic supplies.

BURGHESH TEA ROOM Chiddingstone TN8 7AH (01892 870326) Said to be the oldest working shop in England. Tea and cakes in shop during week, cooked food and more space at weekends: ringing ahead is useful.

TEA ROOMS Chiddingstone Castle TN8 7AD (01892 870347) No entry ticket required to enjoy the rather splendid Victorian tea rooms.

THE ROCK Hoath Corner TN8 7BS (01892 870296) Local ales, hearty food, beamed ceilings, an inglenook fireplace and an ancient 'ring the bull' game make for a perfect country pub.

THE SPOTTED DOG Saints Hill, Penshurst TN11 8EP (01892 870253) Stellar country pub with excellent food and panoramic views over the Medway valley.

THE FOUNTAIN INN Cowden TN8 7JG (01342 850528) Handsome village pub serving good food and beer from the renowned Harveys brewery across the border in Sussex.

The Rock Inn, Hoath Corner

The Spotted Dog

No.4

THE FIFTH CONTINENT

A weekend trip to Kent's mysterious Romney Marsh and Dungeness,
the bleakly beautiful 'land's end' of south-east England

———

'The World, according to the best geographers, is divided into Europe, Asia, Africa, America, and Romney Marsh … In this last-named, and fifth quarter of the globe, a witch may still be discovered in favourable, i.e. stormy seasons, weathering Dungeness Point in an egg-shell, or careering on her broomstick over Dymchurch wall.' So wrote the Reverend Richard Barham in the *Ingoldsby Legends*, a collection of pastiche folklore first published in the 1830s. Barham was for a short time the vicar at Snargate, a fabulously named Romney Marsh village that could be straight out of a Dickens novel or a Tim Burton film. In those days smugglers roamed the marshes, practising their illicit 'free trade' with the continent and sometimes using the churches as secret depots for their contraband; on one occasion customs men made a large seizure of tobacco hidden in the Snargate church belfry. Such stories confirm the view that life here is rarely quite as it seems.

The new high-speed trains to Ashford, which use the same tracks as the Eurostar services bound for Paris and Brussels, make a day out riding on Romney Marsh quite achievable. But my friends and I were up for a little more exploring, so we made a weekend of it with an overnight stay at Rye.

We left Ashford heading south towards Woodchurch, where the tallest thing in the landscape is a handsome white weatherboarded windmill, fully restored to working order. We took in our first view of the marshes from the ridge above Appledore. The land stretched out before us in a patchwork of green and brown, fading to blue where a long line of slowly spinning wind turbines marked the horizon.

This is a continually changing landscape: a thousand years before the Romans arrived it was dense forest, but it has since been a bay and a salt marsh. It's hard to think of a village like Appledore as a thriving medieval port, because today it is nearly ten miles inland, but looking out at this view a thousand years ago it would all have been sea. Appledore and New Romney were on the River Rother estuary and Dungeness was the lonely tip of a long chain of islands, made up of flint gouged from chalk cliffs of the South Downs and washed along the coast by the tides. It's said that the handful of people who lived on Dungeness in those days would sooner sail across to Dieppe than venture up the marshy inlets of the English coastline. A massive tidal surge in the 13th century pushed the river west to Rye and landlocked the towns. Since then, ditches and embankments have transformed the area into rich agricultural land, particularly suited to grazing Romney's own variety of sheep: stocky and handsome, with wool prized for its fineness. Just two centuries ago the marsh was finally drained by the military canal

---

START: Ashford, Kent • FINISH: Ashford (or train from Rye, East Sussex) • DISTANCE: 63 miles/101km
TOTAL ASCENT: 299m • TERRAIN: Quiet lanes, a few busier roads around Lydd and Camber Sands.
Easy over two days, challenging in one.

Rye

Brookland

built during the Napoleonic wars. The reclamation of land was completed soon after, just as the Reverend Barham left Snargate for a more salubrious posting. But throughout the changes the marsh remained a cut-off, dismissed place. People who lived here endured terrible poverty, hardship and ill-health as a result of their damp and diseased surroundings.

It seems unimaginable today, not least because Appledore is an almost impossibly perfect English village. Its long main street is lined with attractive houses and cottages of all sizes and styles, with flower-filled front gardens basking in the sunshine. In the church a flower show was under way, featuring historically themed arrangements, while the village hall was hosting an exhibition of paintings by local artists. A dozen or more club cyclists were soaking up the sunshine on picnic tables outside the pub, while people at the teashop tucked in to towering cakes.

We rolled down into the marsh and on to Snargate. Across the road from Barham's old church is the Red Lion, a tiny pub that dates from the 16th century. Electricity was installed only reluctantly, and the three rooms are illuminated by a single bulb each, with candles in the evening. Refreshed, we disappeared into the narrow lanes that criss-cross the land and stopped at a handful of the 14 medieval churches that are the main historical attraction on the marshes. Each has its own character: first was lonely Fairfield, which stands by itself in the marsh like a ship run aground. Until 1913, when an earthen causeway was built, a boat was needed to reach it, and the key hangs outside a nearby farmhouse. Next was Brooklands with its separate, tiered conical bell-tower, almost as large as the church itself, and finally Old Romney with its soft pink interior, created for *Dr Syn*, a 1960s film adaptation of a novel about a fictional vicar-turned-smuggler.

There are fewer sheep on the marsh than there used to be. The second world war saw them shipped off to Yorkshire and the land converted to arable farming. Even so, saw quite a few, including a small

flock grazing beneath oak and apple trees in a blissful pastoral scene that could have been two centuries ago. Having taken our fill of marshland churches, we turned into a powerful headwind and followed the electricity pylons emanating from the nuclear power station on the beach at Dungeness. Headwinds strip the joy from cycling, reducing it to an exhausting slog, but there was no alternative. We rode together as a compact group and made it to the beach for a picnic tea, sheltering among the upturned boats.

The people who decided to build a nuclear power station at Dungeness apparently thought nobody would come to so isolated and desolate a place in search of pleasure. Since then, the shingle beach has been identified as one of the rarest, most species-rich and most fragile habitats in the country, and the salt marshes inland are now a nature reserve and a haven for migrating birds. The peculiar atmosphere of the place – one of my companions described it as 'less land's end and more end of the world' – has garnered a small following of its own. This is in part because filmmaker Derek Jarman chose to spend his last years here. At Prospect Cottage, a black-tarred fisherman's hut, he created his famous garden of shingle plants, rusty metal and assorted detritus washed up on the beach. The cottage and garden are still there and we took a closer look – but not too close, people do live there! A narrow-gauge steam train chuffed past: at the end of the line are two lighthouses and a pub.

We turned again into the headwind for the long haul to Rye, across the flat marshes and past the tacky holiday resort of Camber Sands. The next morning was spent wandering around Rye, a beautiful little town with steep streets cobbled in pebbles. Somehow it manages to absorb its many visitors without losing any of its authentic, nautical charm. Like Appledore, this was once a busy port, but the changing topography of the area means it's now a couple of miles inland. We rode down to the harbour and along the front, where the shingle beach surrounds a large nature reserve with several birdwatching hides.

On our way back to Ashford we climbed up to the Isle of Oxney, a real island as late as the 17th century,

before the River Rother changed its course to run south of it. It's said that Roman galleys sailing to and from Bodiam stopped off here for feasts. In the church at Stone-in-Oxney is an ancient stone altar with bulls carved on the sides, emblems of the Mithraic cult practiced by Roman soldiers. On the top is a bowl – for the blood of ritual sacrifice? I like to think so.

Leaving Stone-in-Oxney we paused for a final view across the marsh before heading inland. Climate change presents a serious threat as the land now lies on average about 3 ft below the level of the sea at high tide. The shingle wall is the main sea defence, but it is being continually swept eastwards. To slow the changes, the government 'recycles' the shingle, trucking pebbles from east to west every day, from where the waves shift them all, and more, back east again. The timescale is uncertain, but before too long the historic landscape that lay before us may return to the sea once again.

Download route info at thebikeshow.net/04FC

PUBS & PIT STOPS

MISS MOLLETTS HIGH CLASS TEA ROOM 26 The Street, Appledore TN26 2BX (01233 758555) Fancy tea room serving homemade cakes and lunches. Tables outside in fine weather.

THE BLACK LION 15 The Street, Appledore TN26 2BU (01233 758206) Popular pub serving good food in huge portions. Booking advisable, but not possible for Sunday lunch.

THE RED LION Snargate TN29 9UQ (01797 344648) Tiny pub where time stopped sometime in the 1940s.

THE STAR INN St. Mary in the Marsh TN29 0BX (01797 362139) Friendly village pub in the heart of Romney Marsh.

DUNGENESS FISH Battery Road, Lydd on Sea TN29 9NJ (01797 333012) Seafront shack selling locally-caught seafood to take away.

THE SHIP INN The Strand, Rye TN31 7DB (01797 222233) Stylish, cosy pub with good food and rooms for overnight stays.

BIKE SHOP: Spiral Cycles, Station Road, Ashford TN23 1PP (01233 628345)

BIKE HIRE: Romney Cycles, 77 High Street, New Romney TN28 8AZ (01797 362155); Rye Hire, 1 Cyprus Place, Rye TN31 7DR (01797 223033)

Prospect Cottage, Dungeness

No.5

CRAB & WINKLE

A ride through two thousand years of English history in Kent, from Canterbury
to the seaside resort of Whitstable and along the Saxon Shore

---

In times gone by, crossing the channel was a hit-and-miss affair, with at least six places in East Kent to land at or set sail from, depending on the wind and tides. Canterbury grew up as a hub, roughly equidistant between them, with a reliable supply of fresh water. It was the 'capital' for a Kentish tribe as long ago as the Iron Age, then a regional capital for the Romans, and then again for the Saxon tribes that settled here after the Romans left. When St Augustine arrived from the continent, under orders from the Pope, he naturally chose this as the site for his cathedral.

In those days the geography of East Kent was very different. Canterbury's river, the Great Stour, really was great – a broad finger of water reaching west from the the Wantsum Channel, a mile-wide shipping route that linked the English Channel to the Thames estuary. Since the Middle Ages, the channel has silted up and the Wantsum all but disappeared, stranding Canterbury miles from the coast.

When the new technology of the railways came along in the early 19th century, one of the very first lines reconnected Canterbury to the sea, this time along a 6-mile line running north over the hill to Whitstable. Despite its novelty, the Crab and Winkle Line, as it was affectionately known, was never a commercial success and was finally closed in the 1950s. Much of its route is now a cycling and walking path. As we rode uphill out of the city along a path through a park, we looked back at the fine Norman cathedral and imagined how the sight would have thrilled the multitudes of early medieval pilgrims completing their long journeys to the shrine of the murdered archbishop Thomas Becket.

The Crab and Winkle line is surprisingly steep, and this gave the engineers no end of trouble in the early days. For several years they abandoned locomotives and used cables to pull the carriages along; at other times they reverted to dray horses. The hills make it an enjoyable, undulating ride and not the dull, linear experience that is so common on railways converted to cycle paths.

Only a few pockets remain of the huge Forest of Blean that once covered these hills. Many of the trees were felled to fuel the salt-making industry on the coast, which used the simple but effective method of taking sea water and boiling it until only the salt remained. It's easy to see how such an industry can have consumed an entire forest.

Near the village of Blean, the path passes the gate of a tiny 13th-century church, built on the site of an earlier place of worship, that was part of a Saxon manor, in turn built over a Roman villa complex. It's a story of adaptation and renewal

---

START & FINISH: Canterbury • DISTANCE: 32 miles/51km • TOTAL ASCENT: 249m
TERRAIN: Quiet lanes and well-surfaced cycle paths. Moderate.

Whitstable

that's typical of these parts, where one layer of history sits right on top of another. Shortly after the church we passed the high point of the ride, in Clowes Woods, from where it was a long, free-wheeling descent towards the sea.

Despite its growing popularity, Whitstable remains a perfect seaside town. The deep, shapely harbour is surrounded by seafood stalls, there is a narrow high street of colourful independent shops and the long, steep shingle beach is lined by a disorganised assortment of huts and ware-houses, many of them devoted to serving up the town's favourite food: the oyster. The Whitstable Native oyster is highly prized, but the town's oyster festival takes place in late July, when the Natives are out of season. Locals say it's because they are too busy to celebrate during the Native season, but maybe they just want to keep the best for themselves. Rock oysters, fished locally all year round, are tasty alternatives.

Every two years Whitstable holds its Biennale, a festival of cutting-edge visual arts that builds on the town's growing reputation as a cultural centre. We'd timed our visit to coincide with this, and left the bikes locked up while we explored the instal-lations and performances spread out throughout the town. Some of them are in interesting venues: a shack by the beach was hosting a captivating and brilliantly conceived video monologue about a motorway traffic accident.

Back on the bikes we joined the Saxon Shore Way, which runs east along the coast. From Whitstable through Swalecliffe to the far side of Herne Bay is one long beachfront promenade, and it makes for easy cycling with great views out to sea and plenty of places to stop for ice cream. After the long, flat, sea-level ride, helped along by a tailwind, we had to begin turning the pedals a little more purposefully as we climbed the cliffs at Reculver, where a thousand years ago the mainland came to an end.

It was on this headland that the Romans built a fortress defending the north entrance to the Wantsum Channel, looking across it to the Isle of Thanet. Kent's Anglo-Saxon rulers maintained the fort and founded a Christian monastery alongside it in 669AD. Twin towers were added in the 12th century, and today these are all that remain of the medieval abbey, standing magnificently on the cliff edge and serving, if not as a place of worship, as a landmark for passing ships.

Turning inland, we rode south past the wide open, windblown fields of what once would have been the old shoreline, through the small villages of Marshside and Chislet and past the lovely campsite at Nethergong Nurseries. Crossing the Stour at Upstreet we saw several spots for a dip in the river, and had the weather been a few degrees warmer, we'd have jumped in.

Finally turning back towards Canterbury, we rode along the southern edge of the wide valley of the Stour. There were stunning views of the rolling farmland and, in the distance, a shim-mering white expanse of polytunnels sheltering strawberries and raspberries.

Fordwich today has a distinctly sleepy, pastoral

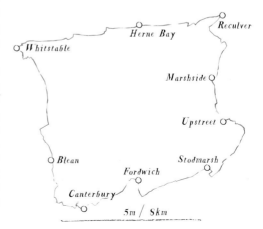

atmosphere, but this but was once a bustling river port. All the stone that was used to rebuild Canterbury Cathedral in the 12th and 13th centuries was quarried in Normandy and landed here, before the river's demise. Inside the old shingle-spired church, which is no longer used for regular worship, is a very large block of limestone carved into the shape of a sarcophagus. It's almost 1,000 years old and part of a shrine to St Augustine, the first Archbishop of Canterbury. After incidents of theft the church is now locked, but the keys can still be borrowed from the Fordwich Arms

pub. From Fordwich we followed a well-surfaced, off-road cycle path along the river and then through the woods back into Canterbury.

A few twists through some housing estates brought us to the heart of the medieval city, where the cathedral towers above narrow, winding streets. Many of these are pedestrianised, not least for the benefit of the hordes of tourists; the latest incarnation of the pilgrims to one of Britain's most historic cities.

Download route info at thebikeshow.net/05CW

PUBS & PIT STOPS

WHEELERS OYSTER BAR 8 High Street, Whitstable CT5 1BQ (01227 273311) Tiny restaurant with an 'oyster parlour' for a swift half-dozen and a glass of Chablis.

JOJO'S 2 Herne Bay Road, Tankerton CT5 2LQ (01227 274519) Oustanding meze/tapas served all day, with a view over the sea.

THE GATE INN Marshside CT3 4EB (01227 860498) Full of character in a lovely location, serving hearty, reasonably priced food.

CHISLET COURT FARM Chislet CT3 4DU (01227 860309) Country house B&B.

NETHERGONG CAMPING Nethergong Hill, Upstreet CT3 4DP (01227 860825) Hard to imagine a better campsite. Tranquil, loads of space, fires allowed, lots for kids to do.

THE RED LION Stodmarsh CT3 4BA (01227 721339) Rural pub, serving good food during lunchtimes and evenings only.

FORDWICH ARMS, King Street, Fordwich CT2 0DB (01227 710444) Beautiful location on the river, decent food.

BIKE SHOPS: Downland Cycles, The Malthouse, St. Stephens Road, Canterbury CT2 7JA (01227 479643); Herberts Cycles, 103 High St, Whitstable CT5 1AY (01227 272072)

BIKE HIRE: Canterbury Cycle Hire, 71 St Dunstan's Street, Canterbury CT2 8BN (01227 388058) Also has branches in Whitstable and Herne Bay, so one-way hires are available.

Stodmarsh

No. 6

THE LONELIEST LANDSCAPE

A spin around the Hoo, a remote north Kent peninsula of wildness, water and wind

———

On a blustery June day a group of friends and I set out from Gravesend with a plan to traverse the Hoo Peninsula, which sits between the Thames to the north and the Medway to the south. We were in search of the 'London Stone' obelisk, which stands in the waters at Yantlet Creek, at the point where the River Thames ends and the Thames Estuary begins. To begin with, we were blown along by the strong westerly wind, and as we rode the weather was moving downstream behind us: harmless paper-white puffs followed by more ominous, towering banks of thunderheads.

The Thames estuary has always been a moody, mysterious place and a favourite haunt of the new breed of psychogeographers, who appreciate the soulful, brooding drama of post-industrial decay and the abandoned military installations that stand out of the flatlands. Each day, water, mud, marsh and dry land are concealed and revealed as the tides rise and fall, and it can be difficult to disentangle past from present, real from imagined.

Hoo is Old English for 'spur of land', and many of the place names here are Saxon, disguised by later spellings. Habitation goes back to the Bronze Age; later the Romans built sea walls and made the first efforts to drain the marshes, and after they left the Jutes arrived from what is now Denmark. But almost more concrete than the Hoo's actual history are its appearances in fiction. Charles Dickens lived in the village of Higham and knew well the 'dark, flat wilderness' that inspired the unforgettable opening scene of *Great Expectations*, in which the young Pip first encounters the terrifying escaped convict Magwitch. A few decades later, Joseph Conrad lived over on the Essex side, and his masterpiece *Heart of Darkness* begins with a powerful evocation of the 'luminous estuary' where 'the sea and the sky were welded together without a joint'.

It's not all foreboding gloom, however. On a bright day the sky is as blue and the sea as gleaming as anywhere else. The gently rolling land and absence of any through traffic makes for fine cycling on lanes that pass by old churches, castles, farms and fruit orchards.

From Gravesend we followed a straight, traffic-free path along an abandoned canal and the railway line as far as Lower Higham, from where quiet lanes hug the edge of the marshes that surround the village of Cliffe. The wildlife seems untroubled by melancholy, and on the route we passed three nature reserves run by the RSPB: Shorne Marshes, Cliffe Pools and (further on, past Cooling) Northward Hill. The last of these boasts the biggest colony of little egrets in Britain, a new arrival to our shores over the past two decades.

START: Gravesend, Kent • FINISH: Strood, Kent • DISTANCE: 30 miles/49km • TOTAL ASCENT: 221m
TERRAIN: Mostly quiet lanes, a couple of busier B-roads and a well-surfaced cycle track. Easy.

Along the way we heard – though we did not catch sight of – croaking bullfrogs and chirruping reed warblers. West of Cliffe, along a long straight track beyond the nature reserve, lies an abandoned fort and near it the impressive remains of the Hans Egede, a wooden vessel beached here half a century ago.

Cooling Castle, with its grandiose twin-towered gatehouse, is hard to miss. It was once the home of Sir John Oldcastle, an early 15th-century religious reformer who was burned at the stake for heresy. These days, Cooling's king of the castle is the boogie-woogie band-leader and television presenter Jools Holland.

It was noon by the time we stopped at the pretty churchyard at Cooling to see the sad line of infant gravestones believed to have been the inspiration for the churchyard in *Great Expectations*. 'Five little stone lozenges, each about a foot and a half long' is how Dickens described the graves of Pip's brothers, set beside those of his parents. Inside the church people were busy setting out huge bowls of strawberries, picked from a neighbouring field, and trays of scones and cakes for a midsummer tea party later that afternoon.

The paved road ends at Allhallows, which was earmarked in the 1930s for expansion into a holiday resort to rival Blackpool. It never happened. We pushed on along the public path over the grassland that leads to the seashore, and then along the water's edge until the London Stone came into view. It marks a historic boundary, the end of the jurisdiction of the City of London, which has been in place since the 12th century, although the current obelisk is more recent. There's another marker, known as the Crow Stone, on the north bank of the estuary near Southend, and a third at the upstream boundary at Staines.

Just across the creek to the south of us lay the Isle of Grain (which was once truly an island, before drainage schemes), with the towering oil-burning power station sitting at the tip of the peninsula. The Medway side of the Hoo is home to two more power stations, a gas import plant and

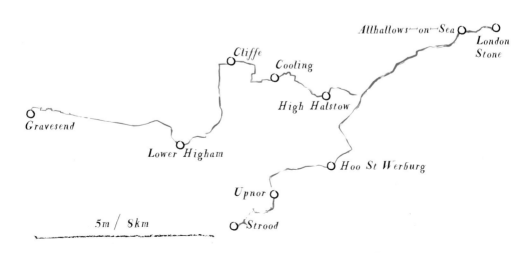

a container port, all supplying the power-hungry economy of the south-east.

We had run out of road and so turned to ride back under the ever-more-dramatic Conradian sky, watching as thunderstorms broke over Canvey Island across the water to the north. Eventually it was our turn, and the dense, dark clouds delivered a freezing and torrential soaking that included a vicious volley of stinging hailstones. We ducked for cover until the storm passed and were grateful for the warm midsummer sun, which brought clouds of steam rising from the road and had dried our clothes by the time we arrived at the pub in Lower Upnor for a very late lunch of fish and chips.

The incongruous juxtaposition of natural wildness and vast industrial developments is part and parcel of the Hoo peninsula's very distinctive atmosphere. There's talk of building an island out into the estuary to house a new London airport dubbed 'Boris Island'. Then again, in the 19th century there was a railway line, now long gone, and plans to create a ferry 'hub' for continental travel.

Who knows what future transformations will be wrought on this strange and desolate landscape? Whatever happens, it will add yet another layer of history to a place that, despite its present isolation, has witnessed the comings and goings of warriors, sailors, merchants and marshmen for as long as people have travelled up and down the Thames.

Download route info at thebikeshow.net/06LL

PUBS & PIT STOPS

THE HORSESHOE & CASTLE Main Rd, Cooling ME3 8DJ (01634 221691) Friendly village pub serving the usual pub food. Three guest rooms for B&B stays.

THE RED DOG The Street, High Halstow ME3 8SF (01634 253001) Pub with a restaurant attached serving Indian food.

THE SHIP INN Lower Upnor E2 4UY (01634 290553) Great location on the banks of the Medway.

THE TUDOR ROSE 29/31 High Street, Upper Upnor ME2 4XG (01634 715305) Popular nautical-themed pub.

BIKE SHOP: Tri The Bike Shop, 18 Windmill Street, Gravesend DA12 1AS (01474 533748)

Cooling Castle

Upper Upnor

Upnor Castle

SUSSEX

THE WILD WEALD

A challenging, roller-coaster ride to the top of Ashdown Forest,
a Sussex landscape steeped in history

———

I was suprised to learn that the High Weald is one of the best surviving medieval landscapes in northern Europe. Sparsely populated, its narrow, sunken lanes run through ancient woods, rising to open heaths and sandstone outcrops and diving into lush, steep-sided valleys known as ghylls. The Weald can feel as wild as anywhere in southern England and it has long served as a place of refuge and sanctuary. During Saxon raids, native Britons fled here from their lowland dwellings, and in more recent times it was a hiding place for high-waymen and outlaws. It's a tough but rewarding place to ride a bicycle: when the road is not going up, it's going down.

We began our journey in the elegant Georgian spa town of Tunbridge Wells and avoided any serious climbing here by riding out past the sandstone crags of High Rocks to Groombridge along the valley of the river Grom, a tiny stream that divides the counties of Kent and Sussex, eventually flowing into the Medway. A steam train plies a short route along the valley. The railway once continued from Groombridge on to East Grinstead, but this branch is now a walking and cycling path. I must confess to mixed feelings about railway paths. They are free of motor traffic, relatively flat and direct: good things for cyclists. But it can be a little be monotonous to

ride through a viewless tunnel of uniform trees and bypassing villages, interesting buildings and other landmarks. There's no sense of place on an old railway line, apart from at the disused stations, whose abandoned platforms have their charm. I also find it difficult not to mourn the passing of these little branch lines, yet another of the seemingly irreversible steps that society has taken towards a car dependency.

Before long, we turned off the railway line to ride into Hartfield, a handsome village with two good pubs, from where several roads lead up towards the top of the Weald. Beyond Newbridge the climbing got serious. Kidd's Hill is a truly vicious ramp that's become a favourite testing ground for local cyclists, who know it simply as 'The Wall'. It begins steeply then eases off, lulling riders into thinking the worst is over. Then, it rears up again for the nastiest section of more than 10% gradient. We made it to the top and only after I'd got my breath back could I appreciate the view, which was astonishing: a big sky overhead and a tapestry of fields and forests stretched across hills that roll away to the horizon – because Ashdown Forest isn't really a forest any more.

The landscape here has changed enormously over the years. Once it was thickly forested, but early Neolithic and Bronze Age farmers cut

---

START & FINISH: Tunbridge Wells, Kent • DISTANCE: 37 miles/58km • TOTAL ASCENT: 917m
TERRAIN: Mostly lanes and B-roads, with a short section of railway path. Challenging.

Ashdown Forest

Ancient yew tree, Rotherfield

Spa Valley Railway

clearings for grazing their livestock and this allowed the heathland to develop. The forests supplied fuel for smelting, the local clay is rich in iron ore deposits, and archaeologists have discovered that primitive ironworking was going on here in pre-Roman times. The combination of dense, wooded valleys and open heath also made the Ashdown ideal for deer hunting, the favourite sport of the medieval nobility. Henry VIII was an enthusiastic hunter, but he also wanted his warships to be equipped with the latest weaponry. As a result, the Weald became the busy centre of the Tudor iron industry. The first cannon forged in England was made at Buxted, on the Ashdown's southern slopes, and place names here tell of the forest's industrial past: Furnace Wood, Five Chimneys, Marlpit Lane, Lime Kiln Wood, Forge Wood. Some streams in the Weald still run red with traces of iron ore in the water.

The felling of trees accelerated, and by the 1630s the last of the ancient woodlands had gone. Without fuel, iron-making moved to the midlands and the north. What was left of the forest was given over to livestock farmers, the soil being too poor for growing crops. Travelling by horse across the Ashdown in January of 1822, the radical journalist William Cobbett described it as 'a heath, with here and there a few birch scrubs upon it, verily the most villainously ugly spot I saw in England'. Since that time, trees have returned to parts of the Ashdown. One of the largest areas of forest is Five Hundred Acre Wood, which was fictionalised as the '100 Aker Wood', home of Winnie-the-Pooh; his creator A.A. Milne lived in the lanes between there and Hartfield.

We continued on up the road, which levels out into a deceptive 'false flat' until reaching the very top of the massif. The government built radio transmitters here during the second world war that were, at the time, the most powerful in the world. They were designed with the express purpose of disrupting German air defences by sending fake instructions to German fighter aircraft. After the war, the transmitters were used by the BBC's Europe service.

There are few roads across the Ashdown and they are straight, encouraging cars to drive faster than they should. Motor traffic increased so much that the free-range grazing of livestock ended in 1985, because too many animals were being lost in collisions with vehicles. There are very few bridleways and cycle tracks through the forest, and local cyclists are campaigning to open more of the existing forest tracks to bicycles.

After a fast run down through Duddleswell, we left the high Ashdown behind and began exploring a series of quiet, narrow lanes. It felt like easy riding to begin with but we were soon cursing how the lanes constantly went up and down as we traversed a succession of steep, narrow valleys. Finally, mercifully, we reached Rotherfield and sat with a cup of tea and a slice of fruit cake in the churchyard, under an ancient yew tree that's split in two and braced with hefty wooden supports.

Inside the church is a stained glass window made by William Morris' decorative furnishings company, featuring assorted saints entangled in a dense forest of Morris' trademark foliage.

Refreshed, we were ready to continue the roller-coaster down-up-down descent to Eridge, arriving just in time to see the steam train puffing away on its short journey to Tunbridge Wells. Much as we might have liked to climb aboard and let the train take the strain, we ended up retracing our tracks of earlier in the day. Tunbridge Wells owes its existence to the iron-laden mineral springs that were discovered there in 1606 by Dudley North, a young English nobleman. Perhaps spotting a potential business opportunity,

North's physician confidently declared the waters a surefire cure for 'the colic, the melancholy, and the vapours'. He boasted that this almost miraculous drink 'made the lean fat, the fat lean; it killed flat worms in the belly, loosened the clammy humours of the body, and dried the over-moist brain.' I was game to see whether the waters could revive the tired legs of cyclists but was told that the spring had recently, and without explanation, dried up. I was assured it was under investigation. The town seemed unperturbed by the news; perhaps because shopping long since replaced the 'taking the waters' as the town's main attraction.

Download route info at thebikeshow.net/07WW

PUBS & PIT STOPS

THE PANTRY Hartfield TN7 4JG (07747 037838) Tea shop in a modernised barn.

THE ANCHOR INN Hartfield TN7 4AG (01892 770424) Cheerful pub serving good food in an unusual timber building. Rooms for overnight stays.

THE GALLIPOT INN Upper Hartfield TN7 4AJ (01892 770268) Cheerful country pub, popular with diners.

DUDDLESWELL TEA ROOMS Duddleswell TN22 3BH (01825 712126) A gem of a tea room known for its home-made scones and cakes.

FORESTERS ARMS Fairwap TN22 3BP (01825 712808) Village pub serving typical pub fare.

CATTS INN High Street, Rotherfield TN6 3LH (01892 852546) Small, unpretentious pub with food, in the heart of the village.

THE HUNTSMAN Groombridge Lane, Eridge TN3 9LE (01892 864258) Large, lively pub with a big garden.

THE CROWN INN Groombridge TN3 9QH (01892 864742) Slightly off route, a lovely Elizabethan free house with good food and very reasonably priced rooms for overnight stays at the start or end of the ride.

BIKE SHOPS: Wild Side Cycles, 77 Camden Road, Tunbridge Wells TN1 2QL (01892 527069); Future Cycles, Lewes Road, Forest Row RH18 5HD (01342 822847)

A QUINTESSENCE OF ENGLAND

Long shadows on cricket grounds, warm beer, old maids bicycling to Holy Communion
through the morning mist: a certain idea of England is alive and well
in the Rother Valley of West Sussex

———

At 112m above sea level, Liphook is one of the higher railway stations in the south east, which makes it a great place to start a bike ride as much of the climbing is done in the train. The town is on the edge of one of the few remaining expanses of the lowland heath that was once widespread across the Sussex Weald. Every spring the woods are carpeted with bluebells, and in summer the displays of purple heather in the clearings are equally spectacular.

Over the past century, most of this kind of land has been lost, either overgrown with forest scrub or cleared for commercial cultivation, but this 300-acre area was saved when local people raised funds to buy it from Viscount Cowdray, one of the biggest local landowners, who put it up for sale in the 1990s. If they had not stepped in, it is likely that the land, used for centuries for communal grazing, woodland coppicing and charcoal making, would have been bought up by commercial timber companies and replanted with fast-growing, non-native species.

From the top of the heath it was a long, satisfying descent to the east into the Rother valley, past picture-book cottages with flower-filled front gardens, the way marked by black and white wooden signposts with tasty-sounding place names like Lickfold and Lurgashall. It quickly became clear that I was riding through the distillation of a certain, treasured vision of rural England: a countryside of

village greens, mill ponds, low-slung village pubs and towering hedgerows. As George Orwell wrote, 'fragments, but characteristic fragments, of the English scene'.

It helped that it was a sunny summer's day, and that the lanes were empty but for the odd person trimming a hedge or devoted to any of the other kinds of pottering that fill the long, idle days of summer in the home counties. My freewheeling came to an end as the lane turned into a sharp ascent on a long, straight lane that leads from Old Mill Farm to the justly named hilltop village of Upperton. Pheasants, with a couple of months of liberty before the guns begin firing in October, were all over the road. Startled at the sound of my approach, they ran clucking and flapping then wheeling over a tall stone wall in their peculiar vertical style of flight, into the sanctuary of the woodland on the other side.

The OS map gives the name of this woodland as Pheasant Copse, and it's part of the grounds of Petworth House, which lies a couple of miles further down the road. Petworth is now partly owned by the National Trust and the 700-acre deer park, landscaped by Lancelot 'Capability' Brown, is open to walkers and cyclists on miles of mostly smooth grass and gravel tracks. Access is from the road that runs south out of the village of Upperton, where the formidable estate walls rejoin the road. Down a flight

---

START/FINISH: Liphook, Hampshire • DISTANCE: 38 miles/60km • TOTAL ASCENT: 624m
TERRAIN: Quiet lanes, with one short, optional off-road track. Moderate to challenging.

The Three Horseshoes, Elsted

St James's, Selham

of steps to the left of the road, beside a gated drive, is a small, unassuming wooden door. It's well worth a look and avoids taking the A272, an unpleasant road for cycling, to Petworth's main entrance. The house (£) is a mecca for art lovers. J.M.W. Turner was a regular guest, and 19 of his paintings hang on the walls alongside others by Van Dyck, Reynolds and Titian. There is also a roomful of the ornate wood carvings of Grinling Gibbons.

Returning to Upperton, I headed west into the up-and-down tangle of little lanes that lead to the village of Lodsworth. These southern slopes were shimmering in the sunshine and are recently planted with vineyards; both changing climate and changing tastes are making English wine an increasingly viable business. From here I could see the South Downs, way off to the south, a blue mass in the haze of the midday sunshine. Once again, I had the feeling I was riding through a perfectly styled vision of the English countryside, and arriving in the picturesque village of Lodsworth I discovered that I was not alone in thinking so.

Lodsworth was the last home of E.H. Shepard, the artist who drew the illustrations for two famous children's books that practically define the English countryside to generations of young readers: Kenneth Graham's *The Wind in the Willows* and A.A. Milne's *Winnie-the-Pooh*. Neither of these books was set in Lodsworth: Christopher Robin and Pooh roamed further east in the Ashdown Forest (*see* Ride No. 7), and Mole and Ratty's river was the Thames (*see* Ride No. 18). And Shepard himself was born in London and still lived there when he produced his classic drawings. But he must have had a vision of the rural England that he wanted to show in his work and when he finally retired to the country, this was the country he chose.

Turning left at his home (adorned with a blue plaque) to the church, next I took my chances along a green lane running downhill, a little bumpy in places, that delivered me to an easy crossing point of the A272, on the lane to Selham, a village that likes to do things small. Selham's Church of St James dates from the 11th century and has been very little changed since then. The herringbone stonework on the outer walls is unusual enough, but the real wonder lies inside, in the intricately carved pillar capitals of the chancel arch: Norman-style curls on one side and serpentine Saxon beasts eating their own tails on the other. Selham's pub, the Three Moles, is one of the smallest in the county and perches on the bank above the road. It was once a railway pub on the now-dismantled Rother Valley line and the multiple CAMRA-awards nailed around the front door confirm the pub's reputation for serving very good beer.

From Selham, I rolled along tiny lanes and into affluent polo country, courtesy of Viscount Cowdray again. The many tenanted cottages on his vast estate have mustard-yellow painted window frames: a brightly coloured reminder of a feudalism that lives on in 21st-century Britain. It seems somewhat subversive that the next village, Heyshott, should celebrate

the radical MP Richard Cobden, who was born here. In the 1830s, Cobden was a founder of the Anti-Corn Law League, the first modern political pressure group. It overturned import taxes on grain that favoured wealthy landowners over working people. *The Economist* magazine began its life as the League's propaganda sheet. Heyshott's village hall is named in honour of Cobden, and there's a memorial plaque on his regular pew in the church.

Heading west, the lanes become narrower as they approach the South Downs. I rode towards the rays of the setting sun past a series of ever smaller and more remote churches. The last of these – the 'Shepherds' Church' at Didling – is a simple building without an electricity supply, relying instead on candlelight. Standing alone in the stillness, the South Downs looming darkly above and an evening breeze picking up ever so slightly, the stark simplicity of these tiny churches struck me as a reminder of how tough life must

have been for those who worked these lands, once so isolated and now so easily reached.

I wanted to linger but knew that I still had some miles to ride, and it was going to be a moonless night. The lanes through Elsted Marsh as far as Chithurst are flat, and I rode on quickly as the first stars emerged among wisps of high cloud in the rapidly darkening sky. From Chithurst the road kicks up abruptly, and dark woods close in overhead. There was still a faint light in the sky, but these steep-banked lanes were inky black with a dark canopy of overhanging trees. I sweated up to the crest of the ridge at Millard, hearing owls hoot and unidentified rustlings in the undergrowth. By the time I rolled into the orange, sodium-lit glow of Liphook I was starving. Sitting on the station platform, I devoured a salty, steaming bag of fish and chips while waiting for the train that would whisk me away from this perfect fragment of England.

Download route info at thebikeshow.net/08QE

PUBS & PIT STOPS

LODSWORTH LARDER The Street, Lodsworth GU28 9BZ (01798 861947) Winner of a national Village Shop of the Year Award, this community-owned shop offers plenty of temping things to eat and drink, and much of it is locally produced.

THE HOLLIST ARMS The Street, Lodsworth GU28 9BZ (01798 861310) Ales from the village brewery, a huge log fire and a French-influenced menu that's a cut above usual pub fare.

THE HORSE GUARDS INN Tillington GU28 9AF (01798 342332) Slightly off route, but worth the detour for good food and stylish, rustic rooms for overnight stays.

THE THREE MOLES Selham GU28 0PN (01798 861303) Award-winning real ale pub serving good, simple food.

THE THREE HORSESHOES Elsted GU29 0JY (01730 825746) Slightly off the route, but good for an afternoon pint, either inside where log fires and candles make for a cosy atmosphere, or outside in the garden with great views over the Downs.

THE ELSTED INN Elsted Marsh GU29 0JT (01730 813662) Attractive country pub with a good reputation for food. Four bedrooms for overnight stays.

BIKE SHOP: Liphook Cycles, 16 The Square, Liphook (01428 727858)

BIKE HIRE: Posh Pedalers, Cowdray Park, Midhurst GU29 0AJ (01730 810889)

St Andrew's, Didling

Upperton Vineyard

TURF & SURF

A seaweedy Sussex adventure from Chichester to West Wittering and Bosham,
across farmland, marsh and sea

———

The beach at West Wittering is just too far away from London for day-trippers in cars, and it lacks a railway station. This could be why it remains the most perfect dune-fringed sandy beach in southern England.

Chichester station lies to the south of the city, and while there's plenty to see in the medieval centre, it's possible to make a quick exit south along the Chichester Ship Canal. Crossing the bridge at Hunston I looked back: this was almost exactly the view painted by J.M.W. Turner around 1828, when the canal was just six years old, a glittering new piece of transport technology. Turner depicts a shadowy 'lighter' boat on the silvery water and a silhouetted ship at anchor, which leads the eye towards the cathedral spire in the distance. Sunset casts a glow over the still evening scene. The view has changed very little since then.

From North Mundham I began a journey across one of the horticultural hotspots of southern England. This low-lying part of Sussex, hemmed in by the sea on three sides, is the Manhood Peninsula, a name derived from *maenewudu*, Old English for 'common wood'. Until the enclosure acts of the 18th century, it was, as the name suggests, common land. Most of the woods are gone now too, and the land is intensively cultivated, with a few pastures for cattle. The rich soil, much of it reclaimed from the sea, and the rain shadow of the Isle of Wight to the south combine to create perfect, sunny growing conditions. Horticulture is big business, with large expanses of land under massive glasshouses and polytunnels.

The lanes are narrow and quiet and wend a wiggling route towards the coast. For some of it roads give way to tracks across farm fields, which can be muddy after heavy rain. But it was quiet, easy riding. Quite unexpectedly, rounding the corner by the Crab and Lobster Inn, the dry land came to an end and I was suddenly overlooking Pagham Harbour, a wide expanse of salt marsh and tidal mudflats.

Sidlesham was once a port of local importance: for many centuries there was a quay here, and a mill that ground corn on the power of the tides. In the 19th century the land was reclaimed from the sea for farming, and the harbour and mill were closed, but only a few decades later the sea breached the defences and the harbour was inundated. Pagham Harbour is now a vast wildlife reserve, a haven for waders and migrating species, the last expanse of wildness on a coastline that's been heavily developed.

Heading west from Sidlesham I was back on tiny lanes through the plant nurseries and market gardens of Highleigh and Almodington, finally

---

START & FINISH: Chichester, West Sussex • DISTANCE: 27 miles/44km • TOTAL ASCENT: 43m
TERRAIN: Quiet lanes and unsurfaced tracks that can get muddy after heavy rain. Easy.

Itchenor Ferry

West Wittering

Bosham

reaching East Wittering. This suburban coastal resort may lack visual charm but still boasts a bustling high street of small, independent shops, where I stopped for picnic supplies. Following the main road into West Wittering, I headed for the beach. If Sussex has a surf culture, this stretch of coast is where it's found. The surf shack was offering board hire and lessons, but the reality is that really good waves are rare, particularly in summer. But there's often a stiff breeze, so wind-surfing, kitesurfing and paddle-boarding are just as popular here as traditional surfing, if not more so.

I continued on to East Head at the very far western end of the beach. This spit of land is a sand-dune paradise, the jewel in the crown of the Manhood Peninsula. It curves around a marshy lagoon that's home to sea lavender and marsh samphire, which autumn had turned a startling blood red. Spiky, blue-green sea holly and pink-and-white-flowered sea bindweed thrive in the sandy soil, and tough, tufty marram grass stabilises the fine sand of the dunes. It's a prime spot for bird-spotting, and twitchers with hefty binoculars were scanning the mudflats for the many species that either live on them or use them as a stop-off on long migratory journeys. Out at sea, small boats sailed to and fro, and I found a sheltered spot among the dunes for a picnic lunch and a snooze before retracing my tracks to West Wittering.

Heading north out of West Wittering, I briefly joined the Salterns Way cycle route along farm tracks towards West Itchenor. From here I took the foot-ferry, which also takes bikes, across the harbour to Bosham (pronounced Bozz'm). The small ferry runs in summer only, and I was the sole passenger on a brief voyage that deposited me on an empty beach, from where it was a short but dramatic ride into Bosham.

Rounding the corner into Bosham's wide, curving, shallow harbour, I saw there was a price to be paid for my dallying at East Head. The tide

was coming in, and I could see that this was a par-ticularly high one. Twice a day, the tide laps the walls of the little cottages that line Bosham's shore, and immediately ahead of me the road leading to the village was already under almost a foot of water. I was faced with the choice of turning back and finding another route or having a go at riding on water. I took a fast run up, but at the deepest point my wheels slowed to a halt and I had no choice but to put my feet down, instantly filling my shoes with seawater.

Cursing my luck I rode into the village and found the pub, where I emptied the water out of my shoes and left them drying by the log fire while I sat out on the terrace overlooking the harbour, watching the tide rise even higher. Maybe I was in good company: according to locals, it was here that King Canute (or Cnut) theatrically demon-strated that the power of earthly kings is 'empty and worthless' compared with the power of God, by commanding the tide to turn back. The tale may be apocryphal, and some say it happened in

in Southampton or Westminster instead. Bosham has other claims to fame: the Bayeux Tapestry depicts King Harold praying under the stone chancel arch of Bosham church before setting sail for Normandy in 1064. His prayers went unanswered as he was captured by William, Duke of Normandy, who then seized the English throne two years later at the Battle of Hastings. The magnificent arch depicted in the tapestry remains the centrepiece of the church nearly 1,000 years later, and debate still rages over whether Harold is buried here rather than in Waltham Abbey.

From Bosham I took farm lanes through fields, avoiding the much quicker but busy A259; despite attempts at a cycle path, this is not a relaxing ride. I couldn't resist stopping in Fishbourne at Barreg Cycles, a brilliantly eccentric bike shop with a yard full of old machines, overseen by a talking parrot. From there I followed National Cycle Route 2 along a quiet back road, past Fishbourne Roman Palace (£), the biggest Roman home in Britain, into Chichester.

What began as a simple trip to the seaside had been an all-day adventure. I could still feel the sea air in my lungs – and the sea water in my shoes – as I boarded the train home.

Download route info at thebikeshow.net/09TS

PUBS & PIT STOPS

THE CRAB AND LOBSTER Mill Lane, Sidlesham PO20 7NB (01243 641233) Foodie inn overlooking Pagham Harbour, with plush rooms for overnight stays.

SPLITS BAKERY 8–9 The Parade, East Wittering PO20 8BN (01243 672309) Traditional bakery, with tables, serving sandwiches.

CALAMITY'S 11 The Parade, East Wittering PO20 8BN (01243 672254) Family-run tea shop.

DRIFT-IN SURF CAFE 11 Shore Road, East Wittering PO20 8DY (01243 672292) Bondi Beach comes to West Sussex in the form of a fun surfer's cafe.

THE LANDING Pound Road, West Wittering PO20 8AJ (01243 513757) Coffee shop and deli serving sandwiches.

THE SHIP INN The Street, Itchenor PO20 7AH (01243 512284) Well-placed pub when waiting for the ferry to Bosham.

ANCHOR BLEU High Street, Bosham PO18 8LS (01243 573956) Cosy harbourside pub, with the back door reinforced against high tides.

BIKE SHOP: Barreg Cycles, Meadowside, Main Road, Fishbourne PO18 8AN (01243 786104)

BIKE HIRE: Coastal Cycles 46a Pier Road, Littlehampton BN17 5LW (01903 730089) Also offers a delivery and collection service.

SURREY,
HAMPSHIRE
& THE ISLE OF WIGHT

WINDSOR GREAT PARK

Traffic-free cycling around the Royal Landscape,
on the border between Surrey and Berkshire

———

For a day's easy riding for children or novice cyclists, there's nowhere in southern England better than Windsor Great Park. Once part of a much larger hunting forest used by Norman kings, today the park covers 5,000 acres – which is still pretty big – and most of it is accessible on smooth, wide, well-surfaced paths shared with walkers, plus a few very quiet roads. I arranged an autumn half-term rendezvous with a couple of friends, one of whom brought her two children, aged six and four, and their little bikes. The five of us set off from the big car park at the Savill Garden: our plan was for a 5-mile southern loop around Virginia Water on the traffic-free paths with the kids, before a second loop for longer legs to explore the hillier northern half with its grand views over Windsor and the Thames valley.

The park is now billed under the name of 'the Royal Landscape'. It boasts some majestic trees, and under a clear sky the golden autumn colours were sensational, but it would take more than autumn colour to keep the kids entertained. Fortunately the Park has hidden surprises around almost every corner, and we agreed that whenever we came upon something special we'd stop for a break and a round of jelly babies.

First of all, there was an obelisk, then a duck pond. Shortly after, and more unexpectedly, a totem pole: a 100ft tree trunk decorated with beavers and eagles in bright colours needed a bit of explaining. Designed by a Kwakiutl chief and carved from a single 600-year-old tree, it was a gift from the people of Canada and marks the centenary of British Columbia, a foot in height for every year of the province's history.

After the totem pole was a very impressive waterfall, where the River Bourne flows out of Virginia Water, at one time the largest man-made lake in the country. The bag of jelly babies was emptying fast. No sooner had we passed the waterfall than I started to think I was seeing things as the most unexpected sight of all came into view: the absolutely genuine ruins of a large Roman temple.

The Corinthian columns and colonnades looked very incongruous nestled into the Surrey countryside. Closer inspection informed us that the ruins were brought to Britain from north Africa nearly two centuries ago. Leptis Magna, once an important Roman city, is in modern-day Libya, and despite being so heavily plundered the ruins there remain one of the most spectacular and unspoilt sites in the Mediterranean.

In terms of the unexpected, a 2,000-year-old ruined temple would be hard to beat. But the surprises just kept on coming, and our young

---

START & FINISH: Egham, Surrey • DISTANCE: 15 miles/24km • TOTAL ASCENT: 189m
TERRAIN: Surfaced paths and a few quiet suburban roads, a little busier through Egham. Easy.

companions were happy riding on, excited to see what would be over the brow of the next hill or around the next bend. We saw a bridge with five arches and a stone chalet that I did my best to convince everyone was home to local witches or gnomes, possibly both, living together in fractious house-share.

On the way back, we rode up a long, metalled tree-lined avenue and were passed by a few cars on their way to the polo grounds. By this point tiredness was setting in, and the four-year-old was riding along in the child seat, his bike strapped to the back of my bike. For a gentle, traffic-free ride it had been about as entertaining as any of us could have hoped and far more exciting than a slog along a disused railway line, which is so often where young children are taken to ride their bikes.

After lunch the remaining pair of us set out for the north of the park, with its long views down to Windsor Castle. We couldn't get over how quiet it was and how much cycling there is, most of it entirely free of motor traffic. Some paths, like the Long Walk down to Windsor Castle, are reserved for people on foot, and that seems fair enough;

there's more than enough of Windsor Great Park to go around. We finished our ride with a visit to the Air Force memorial on Snow Hill and one of the greatest views in southern England from the top, before a steep, white-knuckle descent down a bridleway back to Egham station.

Download route info at thebikeshow.net/10WG

PUBS & PIT STOPS

POST OFFICE, The Village, Windsor Great Park SL4 2HZ. Popular with cyclists, village store serving teas with tables outside.

THE SUN INN Wick Lane, Englefield Green TW20 0UF (01784 432515) Cheerful pub that also hires out bicycles and electric bikes, with optional picnic hampers.

RESTAURANT & CAFETERIA The Savill Building, Wick Lane TW20 0UU (01784 485402) Large, slightly

institutional café and restaurant in an award-winning building whose virtuoso curved roof steals the show.

THE BARLEY MOW Englefield Green TW20 0NX (01784 431857) Slightly off route, but a decent, traditional pub in an area dominated by fancy and overpriced gastropubs.

BIKE HIRE: The Sun Inn (see listing above)

SURREY HILLS LEGBUSTER

So close to London, the Surrey Hills are a magical enclave of quiet valleys, panoramic hilltop views and aerobically challenging cycling between the two

———

Road cycling is booming in Britain and nowhere more than in and around London and the south-east. Cycling clubs like Dulwich Paragon and Kingston Wheelers, which were in slow and apparently terminal decline only a few years ago, now find themselves with record memberships. Along the way the sport had an image makeover, with companies like Rapha offering stylish, high-quality 'race wear' at prices to match. Indeed, such is the popularity of cycling amongst corporate high-flyers that the *Financial Times* has run articles asking 'Is cycling is the new golf?'

British success at the Tour de France and other big races is part of the story, and the 2012 Olympics saw the world's top riders head for the Surrey Hills for a gruelling 155 miles of racing. It was an obvious choice: there are some tough hills, and nowhere is the recent renaissance of road riding more evident than here, from the MAMILs (middle aged men in Lycra) out on Saturday mornings to the Surrey League, which organises one of the country's biggest programmes of amateur cycle racing.

Most people dread riding up hills, but with a little fitness and experience hill climbing can be a satisfying and addictive challenge; there's always the view from the top and the exhilarating descent on the other side to look forward to. Most clubs

round off their summer racing season with a hill-climb event: a race up a short course that lasts barely three minutes. It's one last, lung-stretching, lactic-laden hurrah before the winter break (for the most venerable of all hill climbs, *see* Ride No. 2).

My plan was for a route that crammed as many of Surrey's hills as possible into an energetic half-day ride. Riding out through south-west London didn't seem a fitting start, so I took the train to Effingham Junction, from where a long, straight road leads through Effingham itself and up towards the White Downs. This is the polite way up the White Downs: the climb from the south side is perhaps the most brutal of all Surrey hills and I was relieved to have worked out a route that managed to skip this monster.

I headed west across a patchwork of forest and farmland, and experienced the miracle of modern Surrey: how does a county so close to London, with many large towns of its own, manage to preserve such large expanses of open space with so little traffic on the roads? Not to mention fine villages, like Shere, which I rode through just after crossing the A25, whose sloping streets are lined with dressed-flint cottages and half-timbered houses. Peaslake, a few miles on, is even prettier, and a crowd from the CS Grupetto cycling club

---

START & FINISH: Effingham Junction, Surrey • DISTANCE: 46 miles/74km • TOTAL ASCENT: 1296m
TERRAIN: Country lanes, with short stretch of busier road through Dorking. Very challenging.

Box Hill

Peaslake

Tour of Britain, Leith Hill

were enjoying morning coffee on a grass verge by the rill that runs the length of the main street.

There's something very alpine about this part of the Surrey Hills. It's the clean air, the fragrance of the pine trees, but also the long, blue-tinged vistas to the south, fleetingly framed by trees. From the Regency era onwards, the well-to-do came to the Surrey Hills for picnics, most famously described in Jane Austen's novel *Emma*, where the elaborate picnic on Box Hill ends so disastrously for the book's heroine. The health-conscious Victorians sought the fresh air of the Surrey Hills for its curative powers.

I continued climbing, now on the wooded slopes of Leith Hill. The peak is just short of 1,000ft (300m) in height, but a crenellated stone tower built on the summit in the 18th century cheekily raises it to 1,029ft (314m) to make it the highest point in south-east England. The tower is now managed by the National Trust (£), and on a clear day the views from the top extend to take in 14 counties.

There followed a long, thrilling descent through the woods to Coldharbour and Dorking, along a road with smooth curves, perfect for practising descent technique. The trick is to stay relaxed, planting one's weight on the outside pedal and leaning into the bend to follow a smooth arc through the corner. All the time look well ahead and brake gently on both wheels, before pedalling hard out of the corner to regain any lost speed.

The old market town of Dorking nestles like an Alpine resort beneath steep-sided hills on three sides, and as soon as I was down into the town centre I was riding up again towards Ranmore Common, where I took a turn down to Westhumble and then the famous Zig Zag Road up Box Hill. The Olympic Road Race involved multiple circuits of this hill (nine for the men's race and two for the women's) and the main climb was resurfaced for the occasion. There's no smoother road in England, and it offers not only beautiful views across the wildflower meadows but a road painting by the land artist Richard Long,

inspired by the graffiti that's drawn on the roads during the Tour de France, on the final ramp up to the summit. The gradient is not too steep, and aspiring racers will look to blast up the hill using the big chainring throughout.

By this point I was beginning to flag and had to summon all my willpower for the eighth and last climb, from Westhumble back up to Ranmore Common, from where it was downhill all the way back to the station at Effingham Junction. I'd climbed nearly 1,300m, more than the famous Col du Galibier or Col d'Izoard in the Alps. With a second loop of Box Hill I'd have climbed more than the mighty Col du Tourmalet in the Pyrenees.

Download route info at thebikeshow.net/11SH

PUBS & PIT STOPS

PEASLAKE VILLAGE STORES Peaslake GU5 9RJ (01306 730474) Hot snacks, teas and coffees.

THE KINGS HEAD Pitland Street, Holmbury St Mary RH5 6NP (01306 730282) Real ale, traditional pub food and bar billiards.

TEA SHOP Leith Hill Tower (01306 712711) Tea and cake from a serving hatch in the 250-year-old stone tower.

THE PLOUGH INN Coldharbour RH5 6HD (01306 711793) Home to the Leith Hill microbrewery, with rooms for overnight stays.

NATIONAL TRUST CAFÉ Box Hill KT20 7LB (01306 885502) The ultimate Surrey Hills cycling hangout, for when the hard work's done. Outstanding cakes, though no inside seating.

BIKE SHOPS: Pedal & Spoke, Walking Bottom, Peaslake GU5 9RR (01306 731639); Head for the Hills, 43–44 West Street, Dorking RH4 1BU (01306 885007); Cycles Dauphin, 2 Green Tiles, Box Hill Road, Tadworth KT20 7JE (01737 844576)

No. 12

THE RIPLEY ROAD

Ripley in Surrey was a mecca for London cyclists of the 1890s, and its twice-annual cycle jumble now pulls a crowd of bicycling bargain-hunters.

———

With the spread of railways in the mid-19th century, many of England's roads were suddenly emptied of much of their traffic. The major beneficiaries of these empty roads was a new breed of 'cyclers': courageous young men (and at first, it was only men) astride ungainly pedal-powered contraptions, from big-wheeled penny farthings to bizarre tricycles. These boneshakers were the predecessors of the safety bicycle, which was introduced in the mid-1880s and resembled the modern bicycle of today in all its principal design elements: equal-sized wheels, inflatable tyres and a rear wheel driven by a chain connected to the pedals. Once the basic design was established, the bicycle became immensely popular across society, because it offered new possibilities in fast, self-sufficient and enjoyable travel.

The first London cyclists used their new machines as a way of escaping the smog and grime of the Victorian city, and no weekend route was more popular than the Ripley Road. On May 13th 1894, the police in Kingston-upon-Thames reported 20,000 cyclists passing through *en route* to Ripley, though this may well have been an exaggeration.

In 2012 the Olympic road race saw top bike racers like Bradley Wiggins and Mark Cavendish ride out from central London, passing through Ripley on their way to Box Hill (*see* Ride No. 11). They had the privilege of road closures to protect them from the heavy traffic on the main roads; while it it is possible to follow the Olympic road race route, we opted for the easier option in the form of a train to Woking.

We were on our way to the renowned cycle jumble that the Veteran Cycle Club organises twice a year at Ripley's village hall. A cycle jumble is an odd affair, attracting dealers and collectors as well as ordinary cyclists in the hunt for a bargain – and a fair few attempting to rid themselves of a lifetime of accumulated bicycle clutter. There's always plenty of food available, from bacon sandwiches to formidable slabs of bread pudding, all washed down with steaming mugs of tea. It's a social event as much as anything, a place to catch up on news and gossip among friends.

The ride over from Woking crosses the River Wey. We'd made an early start, and there was mist still rising from the water meadows as the sun rose in a crisp blue sky that was beginning to glow orange and yellow. It was going to be a fine day. At this point, the Wey divides itself into several streams, and standing on an island among them are the ruins of Newark Priory. Its pointed arches mark it out as built in early English Gothic

START & FINISH: Woking, Surrey • DISTANCE: 20 miles/32km • TOTAL ASCENT: 145m • TERRAIN: Urban roads out of Woking, then quiet lanes and a short section of towpath, which can get muddy after heavy rain. Easy.

style, though much of the monastery has been destroyed, mostly by Henry VIII's men, and then by local people who made free use of the stone for mending roads. Better preserved is Pyrford church, an utterly enchanting red-tiled Norman church that crouches on the Woking side of the river. We were on the hunt for bargains at the jumble so didn't stop, but we knew there'd be another chance on our return at the end of the day.

Ripley has the feel of a comfortable country-side outpost set in heart of the Surrey commuter belt. The main road now bypasses the town, and its long high street looks nearly as attractive as it must have been to the cyclists of a hundred years ago. Sadly there is nothing in the Anchor Inn that recalls its colourful past as the cyclists' favourite watering hole. In its heyday, the Anchor was run by two sisters, Annie and Harriet Dibble; when they died, their cycling customers clubbed together to pay for a memorial stained glass window in the church across the road. Also in the church is a brass plaque commemorating Herbert Liddell Cortis, who in 1882 became the first man to ride 20 miles in less than an hour.

Packing away a few vintage bike parts from the jumble, we headed for the quiet rural lanes south-east of Ripley, skimming West and East Horsley before riding along The Drift, a lovely, narrow lane through woods filled with banks of bluebells. The suburban streets of Effingham Junction came as a shock, but soon we were back amongst the woods and fields that are among the 1.2 million acres protected from further development by London's precious Green Belt.

We ventured down an even smaller lane into Wisley Woods, another popular place for cycling in its early years. In the early twentieth century, women cyclists held rallies along these lanes and tracks at around the same time as suffragettes were fighting to get the vote. It was no coinci-dence; women cyclists were at the vanguard of

Cycle jumble, Ripley

the struggle for political and social emancipation. Coincidentally, Ada Lovelace, the early Victorian mathematician who belied conventional views on women's education and wrote what is generally reckoned to be the world's first computer program, lived nearby at Ockham Park.

Crossing the A3 by the pedestrian footbridge we carried on along lanes past the Royal Horticultural Society's famous Wisley garden (£). The garden attracts around a million visitors every year, from casual families to dedicated gardeners. As well as outdoor gardens it has a huge new glasshouse divided into three zones representing desert, tropical and temperate climates.

We were back at the Wey and from the Anchor pub we rode a short distance along the towpath past Pyrford Place, a former home of Elizabeth I and the poet John Donne, as far as Pyrford village. There was time to look inside the Norman church, where areas of red ochre frescoes are preserved amid the whitewash, before returning to Woking. Victorian cyclists said the Ripley Road was 'the best cycling highway in the world'. Those glory days are long gone, but we'd explored some of the delights still to be found in this quiet corner of London's Green Belt.

Download route info at thebikeshow.net/12RR

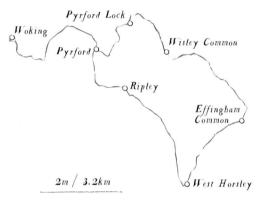

PUBS & PIT STOPS

PINNOCK'S COFFEE HOUSE High St, Ripley GU23 6AF (01483 222419) Specialist coffee shop serving light lunches.

THE KING WILLIAM IV 83, The Street, West Horsley KT24 6BG (01483 282318) Traditional village pub serving local ales and good food.

THE ANCHOR Pyrford Lock, Surrey GU23 6QW (01932 342507) This Anchor has no historical connection with cycling, but it does have a large, sunny terrace on the riverside.

BIKE SHOP: Action Bikes, 2 Chobham Road, Woking GU21 6JH (01483 757376)

No.13

EVERYTHING STOPS FOR TEA

A gentle spin through quiet Surrey lanes with a stop
for the legendary Sunday afternoon teas on Brockham village green

———

Rounding the corner at the top of Box Hill, the magnificent view southwards always comes as a surprise. A cliff so precipitous seems out of place in gently rolling southern England. The steep southern slope of Box Hill has been carved by the River Mole as it flows north from Sussex through Surrey towards the Thames, and for anyone who's spent a few hours of hard riding in the Surrey Hills (*see* Ride No. 11) the flatlands of the Mole Valley are a tempting place to go for a spin.

Perhaps more than anywhere, Surrey encapsulates the potential of lost lanes as a place for peaceful, pleasurable cycling as a much-needed antidote to fast-paced, car-centric life. Despite being crossed by motorways and trunk roads, and sandwiched between Britain's two biggest airports, the county somehow still has plenty of Green Belt land and a network of quiet lanes and tracks over its dramatic hills, open heath and lush, gently rolling farmland.

From Box Hill and Westhumble station we rode south along the separated bike path beside the A24 towards Dorking, past vineyards, then across the main road, through Pixham and up a short, steep, thickly wooded lane. From here it was downhill along narrow lanes winding south through quiet farmland. This area was once part of the huge forest of the Weald, and an early

centre of the Elizabethan iron industry (*see* Ride No. 7). Most of the forest has been felled, though fragments remain in small woods and copses.

As we approached the turn of our route, just north of Charlwood, the biggest change to the landscape lay right ahead of us: Gatwick Airport. In the 1890s, a racecourse was built here, conveniently located beside the London–Brighton railway, with its own station so people and horses could arrive by train. After the first world war, land next to the racecourse was used as an aerodrome for a small flying club, and commercial flights began in the mid-1930s. In the 1950s the airport's future was secured, and more than 30 million passengers now pass through its gates every year.

Heading back north we carried on through small villages along the quietest lanes we could find as far as Leigh (pronounced 'Lye'), where we stopped for lunch at the Plough. The playwright and poet Ben Jonson is said to have lived at Swains Farm, just south of the village, and his portrait hangs in the Seven Stars, a 15th-century pub up the road in Dawes Green where he might have downed the odd pint. Conscious of the need to rebuild our appetites before tea at Brockham, we added a few miles by looping east, over the Mole and up Trumpets Hill, then back over the river just south of the Betchworth Estate.

START/FINISH: Box Hill & Westhumble, Surrey • DISTANCE: 23 miles/37km
TOTAL ASCENT: 240m • TERRAIN: Quiet lanes, with one section of unsurfaced track. Easy.

TEAS

from the Church Hall

2·30 ~ 5·00

WHEELERS LANE

Brockham

Brockham's teas on the village green are held on Sunday afternoons from April to the end of October. Each week volunteers from a different local group or charity bake and sell every manner of cake, flapjack, brownie and scone, and get to keep the proceeds. On our visit it was the turn of the Brockham Young Farmers. Sitting on the green we watched as a gargantuan bonfire was built out of waste wood that had been collected from around the village. Brockham evidently likes to put on a show, and its Guy Fawkes night is one of the best, attracting crowds of up to 20,000 people – nearly ten times the number who live in the village.

We were in the heart of Surrey's commuter belt, yet Brockham has not just held onto its village traditions, it is is positively basking in them. As we prepared to head home, a local cyclist pointed us in the direction of a shortcut, along a path across the golf course, and we rode this way back to Pixham and from there retraced our tracks to the station. Had it not been for that third slice of Victoria sponge I'd have been up for a quick circuit of Box Hill, if only to take in the view across the places we'd just ridden through, but that would have to wait for another time.

Download route info at thebikeshow.net/13ES

PUBS & PIT STOPS

THE SURREY OAKS Parkgate Road, Newdigate RH5 5DZ (01306 631200) Country pub that's won multiple awards for its real ales.

THE PLOUGH Church Road, Leigh RH2 8NJ (01306 611348) Friendly village pub.

THE DOLPHIN INN The Street, Betchworth RH3 7DW (01737 842288) Young's Brewery pub in a pretty corner of Betchworth.

THE SEVEN STARS Bunce Common Road, Dawes Green, Leigh RH2 8NP (01306 611254) Upmarket dining pub.

THE ROYAL OAK Brockham Green, Brockham RH3 7JS (01737 843241) Village pub with a food menu of good-value pub classics.

BIKE SHOP: Head for the Hills, 43–44 West Street, Dorking RH4 1BU (01306 885007)

No. 14

WINCHESTER WINTER WARMER

A ride up the River Itchen to the Iron Age hill forts and
Saxon churches of Hampshire's remote Meon Valley

———

Once the capital of England, Winchester has a history that goes back to pre-Roman times. Despite the best efforts of the 1960s town planners, it retains the street plan laid out by Alfred the Great more than a thousand years ago. It boasts a fine Norman cathedral, a castle, a watermill that was recorded in the Domesday book and idyllic water meadows. We saw precisely none of these as we rolled down the hill from the station and over the River Itchen on a quick and easy route out of town.

We picked up National Cycle Route 23 at a safe if slightly bewildering bridge-and-underpass crossing of the M3 motorway. Suddenly we were on a long country lane alongside the clear waters of the River Itchen, morning mist rising in sun-dappled shrouds. Summer might be the best time for cycling, when the sun is warm and the days are long, but winter has a pleasurable intensity of its own: the bright, low sunshine through skeletal trees; bare, frost-flecked fields; meadows encrusted with sparkling crystal. It was one of those fine midwinter days, and we were all three well wrapped up against the elements. I felt utterly cosy beneath all my layers, and as we rode on, white puffs of our own breath filled the air above our heads. It was barely above freezing, but the sun was bright and the sky was clear and blue; a perfect day to be out for a bike ride.

The Itchen is one of a handful of shallow, fast-running chalk streams that cuts its course through the South Downs. This long chalk ridge rolls south-eastwards for about a hundred miles and comes to an abrupt end at the English Channel, in the white cliffs of Seven Sisters and Beachy Head. Since 2011 it's been Britain's newest National Park. Cycling the whole length is quite possible, though best in summer when the off-road tracks are dry. We continued along empty lanes through Ovington (just before we left Route 23) and Tichborne, following the Itchen to its source just past Cheriton.

On the lanes after Kilmeston we rode through a superb avenue of beech trees. It didn't lead anywhere but it is probable that it's related to nearby Hinton Ampner, a Georgian stately home now owned by the National Trust and best known for its landscaped gardens (£). The house was built after an earlier Tudor hunting lodge was abandoned due to a severe and apparently incurable haunting. One theory is that disgruntled former servants, who had lost their jobs when the new residents brought staff with them, were sneaking back into the house dragging long, heavy chains about during the night.

Without noticing it, we had crossed from the valley of the Itchen into the valley of the Meon. This is now a prime destination for expensive pursuits like trout fishing and golf, but the history of the Meon valley is far more interesting. Not long after the Romans left Britain, settlers from northern Germany and Denmark

---

START & FINISH: Winchester, Hampshire • DISTANCE: 39 miles/63km • TOTAL ASCENT: 632m
TERRAIN: Quiet lanes and surfaced cycle paths, one section of main road. Moderate to challenging.

East Meon

began to arrive along the south coast. In these hills, Jutish tribes from northern Denmark intermingled with native Britons, and the Meonwara were among the last people in England to be converted from paganism to Christianity, a testament to the remoteness of the area in those days.

Soon after, lands in the Meon valley were given to the Bishop of Winchester, and this prestigious connection resulted in the building of some fine churches, All Saints in East Meon being the most impressive. It is set on a slight hill, and its stocky Norman tower with a witches-hat spire looms over the village. Zigzags characterise the building, from the leading on the spire to the arches on the tower windows and side door.

Inside, the chief attraction is a black marble font carved in the 12th century in Tournai, now part of Belgium. It is a superb piece of work, like nothing I'd ever seen. The font is one of only seven brought to England by Henri of Blois, grandson of William the Conqueror. Standing in the church and looking at this huge, dark block, it was hard to imagine how it was sailed across the channel to Southampton, then up the Itchen before being carried the rest of the way overland. From East Meon we rode up a

short, steep climb to Teglease Down. From the top, the sail-like Spinnaker Tower at Portsmouth, 12 miles south, was clearly visible in the bright midday haze. Beyond, the Solent gleamed in a long strip of silver and the humpbacked hills of the Isle of Wight (*see* Ride No. 15) rose in the very distance. In the other direction was Old Winchester Hill, its summit crowned by the earthwork ramparts of an Iron Age hill fort.

We rode fast downhill to Meon Stoke and through Corhampton, whose lovely Saxon church (built in 1020 and little changed since) crouches on a mound above the road, next to an even older spreading yew tree. Inside the church are the traces of wall paintings that are over 700 years old.

My companions were beginning to suspect that my interest in Saxon church architecture was a crafty ruse to put off the inevitable monster climb out of the Meon Valley. They may have been right. Beacon Hill is a notorious climb, rising 133m with an average gradient of 5.5%, a statistic that conceals a brutal middle section of double-digit gradients that compel all but the sturdiest mountain goats to get off and walk. Nothing wrong with that, of course: all the better to enjoy the view.

From the top it was a long, undulating run until we met up with the A272, a main road that's unavoidable but wide enough to ride safely, especially as it's a gentle downhill that is over fairly quickly. Anyone with a bike equipped for off-road adventures will be able to follow the South Downs Way instead, along tracks and bridleways.

Our approach to Winchester was along the dead-straight Alresford Road, and our route into into the historic city was every bit as spectacular as our exit from it had been mundane. We stopped to warm up with a pint by the log fire at the Black Boy pub, before a quick tour around the precincts of the vast Gothic cathedral, where a Christmas fair was in full swing. The cathedral is one of the largest in Europe and its long, high vaulted interior is quite breathtaking (£). The original medieval stained glass of its huge west window was smashed by Cromwell's forces during the Civil War, then randomly pieced back together in an early form of collage. There's also a chapel with lovely stained glass windows by William Morris' Pre-Raphaelite Brotherhood.

Heading up the hill to the station, I paused by the Westgate, a medieval fortification built on the site of the original Roman city gateway. The Westgate once housed a debtors' prison, but is now home to a free museum of Winchester history. It seems incredible that until 1959 all traffic entering or leaving the city had to pass through this narrow archway. Winchester's post-war civic leaders put the car first, widening roads and demolishing buildings, including part of the Westgate. The tide has since turned again and Winchester, like many towns and cities, is now re-civilising itself by reclaiming space from cars to allow people to get around the city more easily on foot or by bike.

Download route info at thebikeshow.net/14WW

PUBS & PIT STOPS

TICHBORNE ARMS Tichborne SO24 0NA (01962 733760) Thatched free house serving ales straight from the barrel.

THE FLOWERPOTS INN Brandy Mount, Cheriton SO24 0QQ (01962 771318) Serving beer from the small brewery next door. Rooms for overnight stays.

TAZZINA High Street, West Meon GU32 1LJ (01730 829882) Tiny café with a garden serving breakfast, lunch and homemade cakes (closed Sundays in winter).

YE OLDE GEORGE INN Church Street, East Meon GU32 1NH (01730 823481) Village pub serving above-average pub food. Rooms for overnight stays.

THE SHOE INN Shoe Lane, Exton SO32 3NT (01489 877526). Handsome pub serving elaborate, locally sourced food.

THE BUSH INN Ovington SO24 0RE (01962 732764) Top-quality food, sunny garden in summer.

THE MILBURYS Beauworth SO24 0PB (01962 771248). Old-fashioned country pub with a massive treadmill for a 300ft well, and a skittle alley.

BLACK BOY 1 Wharf Hill, Winchester SO23 9NP (01962 861754). Wonderfully eccentric pub with all manner of strange objects on display. Hearty food and log fires in winter.

BIKE SHOP: Hargroves Cycles, 10 City Road, Winchester SO23 8SD (01962 860005)

BIKE HIRE: Bikeabout, Winchester Tourist Information Centre, High Street, Winchester SO23 9GH (01962 840500)

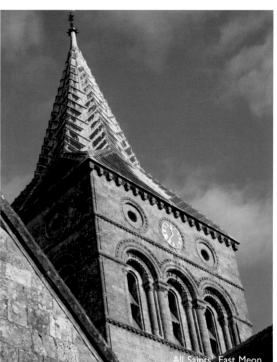

All Saints , East Meon

Teglease Down

No. 15

AROUND THE WIGHT

A weekend's circumnavigation of the Isle of Wight shows there is much more
to England's largest island than rigging and regattas

———

It's a surprise how many people spend their lives in southern England without ever finding out what's at the other end of a 20-minute ferry ride. Cut off from the mainland, the Isle of Wight is a world unto itself: gentler, slower and more intensely scenic than anywhere else on the south coast. According to the meteorologists, it's also England's sunniest county. It seems possible that the island's inhabitants and regular visitors prefer to keep the secret to themselves.

For the uninitiated there's no better way to discover the island than by riding around it on a bicycle. At nearly 70 miles – many of them hilly – it makes for a challenging day ride for a fit rider. But it's even more rewarding when ridden as a miniature cycle tour: this was my plan as as I disembarked the speedy catamaran from Portsmouth Harbour with a tent, a stove and a sleeping bag stuffed into my panniers and set off towards Ryde, my wheels rumbling along the long wooden pier.

Ryde itself doesn't make for an attractive start, with its feeling of having seen better days, a sad promenade of dingy amusement arcades and the aroma of fried food hanging in the air. I pressed on along the main road, which was the only real option, but it should be stressed that main roads on the island are way calmer than those on the

mainland. On the outskirts of the pretty town of Seaview I joined a round-the-island cycle route that is well marked with blue-and-white signs, making navigation a doddle.

Bembridge harbour was where I finally encountered the real seaside, in the form of a wide estuary full of colourful boats and hundreds of sea birds wheeling in the air or picking over the mudflats for tasty morsels of shellfish. I found a little more than a morsel at the excellent fishmonger: a whole dressed crab that I matched with a crusty loaf of bread from the bakery. Bembridge is famous for its crustaceans: they say the clear water and shallow reefs prevent the crabs and lobsters from growing too big and losing their sweetness.

On the way out of Bembridge is the only surviving windmill on the island, now maintained by the National Trust as a museum of milling (£). It was built in the early 18th century, when the town was really just a muddy assortment of wooden huts and farmhouses that was almost entirely cut off by water from the rest of the Wight. Land reclamation improved matters, but the village only grew up in the late 19th century, when the island became a popular holiday destination – most famously, Queen Victoria spent her summers at Osborne House, just outside Cowes.

START & FINISH: Ryde, Isle of Wight • DISTANCE: 68 miles/109km • TOTAL ASCENT: 1,048m
TERRAIN: Mostly quiet lanes with a few short stretches of busier main roads and a 2 mile/3km riverside
cycle path. Challenging in a single day, moderate in two.

Compton Farm

Development brought connections with the wider world, and imported flour eventually put the windmill out of business. It ground its last corn in 1913. Most of the machinery remains intact, and I scaled the rickety wooden ladders while an audio tour explained how it all worked. As I took in the panoramic view from the top, the old wooden machinery creaked and groaned all around me in the gusty winds.

The road rolls on – up and down and up again – to Brading. Just outside the town are the preserved remains of a courtyard villa from the earliest days of Roman Britain (£), which may have been the site of one of the first vineyards in the British Isles. Fittingly, on the southern slopes of Brading Down lies Adgestone Vineyard, one of the very first of the modern vineyards now found across southern England, planted in 1968.

That same year, just a few miles up the lane, the first Isle of Wight music festival saw 10,000 people gather at Ford Farm, near Godshill, for a line-up that included Jefferson Airplane and T-Rex. Two years later, the festival drew 600,000 people to the chalk hills of Afton Down near Freshwater. This was the biggest musical event of the decade, bigger than Woodstock, with a line-up that included Jimi Hendrix, The Doors, The Who, Miles Davis, Joan Baez and Free. Festival-goers outnumbered island residents by an extraordinary six to one. If the numbers are hard to grasp, the Glastonbury festival pulls in a comparatively measly 150,000 or so every summer, and the more recent, revived Isle of Wight festivals closer to 50,000.

From Alverstone I began the biggest climb of whole mini-tour, all the way up through Wroxhall to a clifftop road high above Ventnor Bay, with dramatic views out to sea. After descending to Whitwell it was up once again through Niton and then up the southern slopes of St Catherine's Hill, the high point of the entire coastal route. Looking ahead from the top, I could see the western half of the island laid out like thick green carpet that met the sea in a line of low brown cliffs. I fairly flew down the hill past Blackgang Chine to Chale.

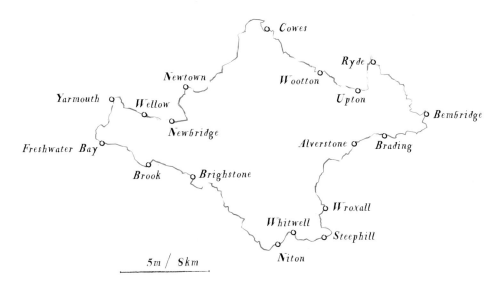

This southerly tip of the island was notorious for shipwrecks, with dangerous underwater reefs and sea fogs that blotted out the warning signals from lighthouses. The dark 'chines' – fern-hung ravines at the river mouths of the area – also earned an unsavoury reputation for smugglers and 'wreckers': unscrupulous folk who tricked passing ships onto the treacherous rocks to plunder their cargo. Looking back up to St Catherine's Hill I could just pick out the tower of St. Catherine's Oratory, also known as the Pepperpot. It is said to be Britain's oldest medieval lighthouse, though it may actually have been a chapel bell tower with a beacon built beside it. The local story says that it was built in 1323 by Walter de Godeton, in penance for having scavenged wine from the wreck of a ship that ran aground in Chale Bay. The wine belonged to a monastery, and the religious authorities threatened de Godeton with eternal damnation unless he made amends somehow.

From Chale to Freshwater is the most remote and least developed part of the island. A coastal road was built for the military in the 1860s but remained in private use for 70 years. The present road was built in the 1930s and is now quite fast in places, so I was glad to divert inland onto quiet farm lanes, empty but for the occasional tractor that sent me heading for the verges to get out of the way. The hedgerows were filled with blackberries and I stopped now and again for a handful of nature's tastiest energy snack. Brighstone and Mottistone are perfectly preserved countryside villages and seem almost unaware of the sea just a mile away.

At Brook I rejoined the modern world for an unavoidable stretch on the main coast road. Ever since it was built, the road has fought a losing battle with the forces of coastal erosion. Experts say within a few years large sections will lost to the sea, and the authorities are debating what to do. One option is to let nature take its course and convert what's left of the road into a pair of cul-de-sacs reached from inland roads. A more radical plan is for a new 'coast' road along the top of the Downs, a move which would surely ruin one of England's most breathtaking stretches of countryside.

As the sun dipped over the sea, I pitched my tent at Compton Farm, a small family farm with an equally small campsite. The farm is home to cattle and sheep, plus some lively geese who inhabit a pond just in front of the old stone farmhouse. It is conveniently situated right next to Compton Bay, easily the best beach on the island and as popular with surfers as it is with swimmers.

The chalk grassland here is low in natural fertility, which makes it perfect for wildflowers. Now, near the end of summer, the meadows along the coast were turning brown and studded with dark seed-heads, including the most spectacular drifts of teasel I have ever seen. I promised myself I'd come back in the early summer to see them in their glory. These beautiful meadows are sown by the local farmers and grazed by their animals. It's an ecologically harmonious relationship, but probably not as profitable as the gigantic field of heavily sprayed cauliflowers I had passed a few miles back.

The next day I left my tent and bags at the campsite and spent the morning exploring the tracks and bridleways high up on the Downs on a bike free of panniers, before continuing to Freshwater Bay, where the steep shingle beach and towering chalk cliffs make for a lovely swimming spot. When big waves roll in, the sound of thousands of pebbles shifting can be almost deafening. It was at Freshwater Bay that Alfred Tennyson heard the 'scream of a maddened beach dragged down by the wave'; his home, Farringford (now a hotel), sits on one of the hills above the bay.

From the Red Lion pub in Freshwater a wooded track runs along the River Yar to

Yarmouth. This is a town with a distinctly nautical air, from the ships' chandler's full of rope and polished brass to the long wooden fishing pier with its hexagonal shelter. The harbour is home to one of the island's lifeboat stations, and the last of Henry VIII's coastal 'castles', a squat blockhouse at the entrance to the harbour (£).

From Yarmouth I turned inland once again, riding along quiet lanes through farmland around Wellow, where busy preparations were underway for a ploughing match the next day. After dodging yet more tractors coming down the lanes towards me, I found myself back at the sea in Newtown, a place with an exceptionally misleading name. Probably founded before the Normans arrived, until the 14th century it was a thriving port and the biggest town on the island. Then it suffered French raids from the sea and an outbreak of the plague, and finally its harbour began to silt up. Today, Newtown is just a small hamlet of a few houses with an Elizabethan town hall that's open to the public (£). The town hall was bought, restored and donated to the National Trust by the 'Ferguson's Gang', a mysterious band who, in the 1920s and 1930s, set about preserving the English countryside from destructive development. They had a lot of fun in the process, wearing masks and using pen-names to conceal their true identities, but they are believed to have been a group of wealthy and well-educated young women. Bright Young Things, certainly, but well-intentioned and surprisingly effective.

By this point the sunshine had gone and dark clouds were gathering in the Solent. I sensed a storm approaching and started to look for a place to spend the night. A little farther along the coast I rode down a track to a quiet beach and put my tent up on the edge of the sands. I dived in just as the thick grey clouds that had blotted out the sun opened with a ferocious fifteen minutes of summer rain. As I heated up some soup in my tent,

River Yar

Brighstone Down

133

I watched the sun appear one last time from below the clouds before sinking over the horizon.

It was a cold night, and the morning sky was a clear deep blue as I rounded the headland and rode into Cowes. I picked my way through the town, crossing the fast flowing river on the chain-ferry, and continued apace through gritty East Cowes and past St Mildred's church in Whippingham, an outlandish fantasy of Gothic revival built for Queen Victoria and Prince Albert, who is said to have had a hand in its design. Following a back-road through Wootton, I crossed the bridge and rode the remaining forested hills before descending into Ryde. A distance that could be a good day's ride had yielded much more as a three-day camping adventure. More than anywhere in southern England, the Isle of Wight is a place that rewards people who take their time.

Download route info at thebikeshow.net/15AW

PUBS & PIT STOPS

NORTHBANK HOTEL Seaview PO34 5ET (01983 612227) Favoured by the photographer Martin Parr, this archetypal seaside hotel rises above the chintz to make for an entertaining step back in time.

THE OVERBOARD Bembridge Harbour, Embankment Road, between St Helens and Bembridge (07582 457049) Seasonal café in a boat serving fairly standard fare in an unusual setting.

OCEAN VIEW 1 Newport Road, Ventnor PO38 1AE (01983 852865) Quality fish and chips with a fine view from the cliffs above the town.

THE BUDDLE INN St Catherine's Road, Niton PO38 2NE (01983 730243) Slightly off-route, but this historic pub full of nooks and corners is worth the detour.

SEVEN Main Road, Brighstone PO30 4AH (01983 740370) Elegant café/bistro in a pretty village, which also does B&B.

THE SUN INN Hulverstone PO30 4EH (01983 741124) Last pub before Freshwater makes this a popular choice.

COMPTON FARM CAMPSITE Military Road, Brook PO30 4HF (01983 740215) Free-range campsite open April to September.

THE RED LION Church Place, Freshwater PO40 9BP (01983 754925) Lovely village pub in an idyllic setting at the top of the River Yar estuary.

THE GEORGE HOTEL Quay Street, Yarmouth PO41 0PE (01983 760331) Push the boat out at this splendid but pricey hotel with a fantastic view across the Solent.

GOSSIPS CAFE The Square, Yarmouth PO41 0NS (01983 760 646) Locals' favourite, right by the pier with good sea views.

THE NEW INN Main Road, Shalfleet, PO30 4NS (01983 531314) Slightly off-route, a deservedly popular foodie pub well worth the detour.

BIKE SHOPS: TAV Cycles, 140–140a High Street, Ryde PO33 2RE (01983 812989); Wight Mountain 31 Orchard Street, Newport PO30 1JZ (01983 533445)

BIKE HIRE: Wight Cycle Hire, The Old Works, Station Road, Yarmouth PO41 0QU (01983 761800)

THAMES VALLEY

ESCAPE TO COOKHAM ISLAND

A lazy, watery weekend ride to a tiny riverside campsite near Cookham in Berkshire, the Thames village where Stanley Spencer lived and worked

———

A summer heatwave was on. We needed to get out of the city, away from the traffic – and for more than just a day. We wanted to spend a night under the stars, but not in a big campsite full of cars and caravans. Most people know that riverside paths are great places for bike rides, particularly in summer, when life on the water is buzzing and a quick, refreshing dip is always a possibility; less well-known is that a handful of locks have small campsites reserved for those arriving by boat, bicycle or on foot. Our destination was one of these: the lock at Cookham, the Thames village immortalised by painter Stanley Spencer, who was born and lived most of his life there.

We lugged the two bikes, mine loaded with the camping gear, off the train at Iver, just beyond the M25, and were quickly riding along a quiet stretch of the Grand Union Canal. Britain's canals are extraordinary feats of engineering and construction, built by tens of thousands of labourers with just hand shovels. Yet their time as the major arteries of trade and transportation was fleeting. In many instances, their last profitable work was to move the materials for building the new railways, the direct competitors that would put the canals out of business. Slough was a tiny village until those railways came in the mid-19th century and sparked its development into a large industrial town.

The canal was deserted, and under the blue sky it felt like a long green shoot reaching into the unlovely eastern suburbs of the town. The rattle of our bikes broke the quiet and must have disturbed a heron standing sentry on a half-submerged branch. It spread its wings and with one spring of gangly black legs and a gentle flap of wings, launched into flight, gliding gracefully over the water before banking to the right and rising up into the canopy of trees, safely out of sight.

Soon after, we joined National Cycle Route 61, which comes down from Watford, and left the canal behind. Following the blue signposts south, we wound through the rabbit warren of Slough's post-war housing estates. It felt a long way from Spencer's paradise by the Thames, but soon enough the route turned into a traffic-free path that delivered us painlessly over the A4 and into Ditton Park. The park dates back a thousand years, but the present grounds were laid out in in the 18th century by Lancelot 'Capability' Brown. The boffins of the Radio Research Station were based there in the 1930s when they first started working on using radar to detect aeroplanes, work that paid off during the Battle of Britain.

In fine sunshine, we followed the path through wide expanses of cricket pitches and football fields and then over the M4 to the Jubilee River,

---

START: Iver, Bucks • FINISH: Slough, Berkshire • DISTANCE: 32 miles/51km • TOTAL ASCENT: 157m
TERRAIN: Riverside paths, country lanes, woodland tracks and a few urban roads. Easy.

which flows from Maidenhead to Windsor. Maps from the last century don't show the course of this wide river, parallel to the Thames, because it didn't exist until 2003. It was built as a flood diversion channel, and at the time was the largest man-made river in Britain, the second largest in Europe. During its construction, reed beds and wet woodland were laid down, and a quarter of a million trees were planted. As a flood defence system it was found not to work very well at first, and the Environment Agency successfully sued the lead contractors for the cost of improvements. It makes for a fine cycle route; the only downside is the rumble of the M4 motorway, which, like the canal and the railway before it, follows the course of the Thames valley.

It required some careful map-reading to pick our way across Maidenhead and find the newly designated National Cycle Route 50, which follows a good but unsurfaced path over the fields to Cookham. The A4049 main road is not too bad as an alternative for anyone who isn't inclined to track down the quieter but more fiddly cycle route.

There can be no question that Cookham is a delightful village, with its black-and-white houses with red-tiled roofs, each building a little different from the next. But it was high summer and so utterly choked with cars, both parked and moving, that we found it difficult to appreciate Spencer's 'village in Heaven' for what it really is.

We found the serenity we were looking for down by the river, arriving at the lock in time for an ice cream from the little kiosk before unpacking. The lock and campsite are on an island, and there are only eight pitches. We put our little tent right at the tip of the island, with a wide stretch of river outside our front door. Compared with the roads, river traffic is slow and quiet, and we watched craft of all kinds, from white glass-fibre gin palaces to painted narrowboats, negotiate the lock on their weekend journeys.

Grand Union Canal

The next morning I woke early for a swim in the still, unbroken water, as the sun rose above the trees and dried the night's dew from our tent. After breakfast we popped in to have a look at the Stanley Spencer gallery (£), a highlight of which is his giant, unfinished canvas *Christ Preaching at Cookham Regatta.*

Our previous day's ride had been just 17 miles without so much as a molehill, but it couldn't last, and the morning began with a tough ascent up the gorge cut by the Thames as it rounds the south-western spur of the Chilterns. The climb passes the main entrance to Cliveden House, an opulent country house that was doubly notorious in the 20th century. Between the wars it was the home of Nancy Astor and the 'Cliveden set', a cabal of aristocratic right-wingers who sought friendlier relations with Nazi Germany. In the 1960s the house provided the glittering backdrop to the Profumo Affair, a story of sex, lies and Soviet spies that shook the British establishment to its core. Today the extravagant gardens and some of the rooms in the house are open to the public under the ownership of the National Trust (£).

Up on Littleworth Common, river life was left far behind. We were now rolling along quiet forest lanes, which became wilder still as we left the road for a short run on well-surfaced tracks through Burnham Beeches. There are 500 acres of ancient woodland here, saved from development by Victorian social reformers who felt the working people of London needed open spaces they could enjoy. How right they were.

Rejoining the road we headed on a roundabout route to the church of St Giles in Stoke Poges. The large churchyard, with its lichened gravestones and pathway lined with roses, is thought to be the setting of Thomas Gray's *Elegy Written in a Country Churchyard.* In 1759, a poetry-loving general of the British army fighting the French in Canada is said to have recited the poem to his officers on the eve of battle, adding, 'Gentlemen, I would rather have written that poem than take Quebec tomorrow'. Still considered among the finest of all English poems,

it contains, according to one critic, 'more famous quotations per linear inch of text than any other in the English language, not even excepting Hamlet', many of which have since passed into cliché.

Gray is buried in the churchyard, and extracts of his poem are carved on a bulky, neoclassical stone memorial that stands in a meadow next door. I suspect that Gray, who was a sensitive soul, would have hated such a vulgar lump. Tuning out the hum of traffic away in the distance, it is still a tranquil setting. The church is also known, among cyclists, for its curious stained-glass 'bicycle window' which shows a naked figure riding what looks like an early wooden bicycle and blowing a long trumpet. Fully clothed and with no trumpets, we were back on the road for one of the most dramatic changes of scenery I've ever experienced on a bicycle: from the quiet country lanes of Stoke Poges to the concrete boulevards of Slough, and a train home.

Download route info at thebikeshow.net/16EC

PUBS & PIT STOPS

THE PINEAPPLE Lake End Road, Dorney SL4 6QS (01628 662353) Famously gargantuan sandwiches and a good selection of beers. A wood-burning stove in winter and a garden for sunny days.

THE CROWN The Moor, Cookham SL6 9SB (01628 520163) Well-placed for enjoying a sunset drink by the large village green. Serves decent food.

THE OLD SWAN UPPERS The Pound, Cookham SL6 9QE (01628 521324) Small village pub, named for historic annual census of swans on the Thames. Two rooms for overnight stays.

COOKHAM LOCK Cookham SL6 9SR (01628 520752) Camping from April to October, bookings by phone.

THE JOLLY WOODMAN Littleworth Common SL1 8PF (01753 644350) Friendly pub serving a menu of local food including its own homemade pies.

BLACKWOOD ARMS Littleworth Common SL1 8PP (01753 645672) Small, well-preserved pub in a quiet spot on the edge of the Chilterns.

WHITE HORSE Hedgerley SL2 3UY (01753 643225) A good, old-fashioned county pub with cosy interiors, a garden and uncomplicated, homemade food.

BIKE SHOPS: Cookham Cycles, Cookham SL6 9BR (01628 530505); On 2 Wheels, Bourne End, SL8 5QN (01628 533 003).

Cookham

Burnham Beeches

No. 17

A THAMES MEANDER

Starting in Reading, an exploration of the upper Thames, from millionaires' riverside palaces to quaint thatched villages, including a climb through the quiet, wooded lanes of the Chilterns and on into Oxfordshire

Reading is the first stop on the express trains heading west out of London, which makes it an excellent jumping-off point to explore this part of the Thames valley; we had packed swimming gear and food and drink for a picnic by the river before heading up a few hills. As a town of 150,000 people Reading is undeniably urban, but the Thames runs right through its centre and provides an excellent route into the surrounding countryside. From the railway station it was just a few hundred yards down to the river, from where there's a choice between turning left towards Pangbourne and the Berkshire Downs (*see* Ride No. 18) or right through the pretty towns of Sonning and Shiplake.

We turned right and followed the Thames Path, keeping the river to our left and ignoring blue signs for National Cycle Route 4, which heads inland from the river and is a much less pleasant ride. As ever when sharing a path with walkers, we took it easy slowly and gave polite rings of the bell to alert people out walking that we were about to pass. The path as far as Sonning is flat, hard-packed gravel and quite passable on any bike and at any time of the year.

After a coffee and cake in the bunting-bedecked tea garden at Sonning Lock, we followed the Thames Path over Sonning Bridge. This is an ancient crossing point of the Thames

where it once marked the boundary between the old English kingdoms of Wessex and Mercia. In the scheme of things, the present bridge is relatively young, built in 1775. Across the bridge, we continued riding downstream on the other (north) bank of the river. On this side, the Thames Path is narrower and less well-surfaced and feels altogether wilder. Marsh-loving teasels towered overhead, and we caught glimpses of the river through the thick vegetation. There are plenty of swimming spots along here, but we kept going.

The Thames Path takes a brief diversion through Lower Shiplake at Shiplake Lock; some of the most expensive homes in the country are along this stretch of river, and their gardens sweep right down to the water. Particularly ostentatious are the manicured grounds of Thames Side Court, owned by Swiss multi-millionaire financier Urs Schwarzenbach, which are laid out complete with a model railway and a scale model of the train station at St Moritz, much of it visible from the path as we rode past.

Soon after passing this miniature Switzerland we were back onto the Thames Path for the riverside run-in to Henley-on-Thames and found the perfect picnic spot: a grassy glade right on the bank of the river with plenty of shady space for lounging about. I was in the water with a splash,

START & FINISH: Reading, Berkshire – Didcot, Oxfordshire • DISTANCE: 35 miles/57km • TOTAL ASCENT: 357m • TERRAIN: Riverside path (parts can be muddy after heavy rain), quiet lanes. Moderate.

145

the others following me in. Drying off in the sun, we emptied our panniers and arranged a huge picnic spread. The thermometer was edging towards 'scorcher', and we were only too happy to take it easy for a while.

When we finally got moving again, the approach to Henley involved dismounting and pushing our bikes along timber pontoons over a weir complex, with stunning views over the river on all sides. Henley was heaving: ice creams, sunbathers, picnics, dogs and kids running all over the place, games of frisbee and football and all the other things people like to do on a summer day down by the river. Riding into the centre of Henley, we turned our backs on the river for a long ascent that began with a steep climb of about a mile before it flattened out a little.

Beyond Peppard Common were some of the quietest lanes in the area, with wonderful runs through towering forests, climbing gently up to the highest point of the ride at Stoke Row. On our right was a very unlikely sight for a small village in the Chilterns: an elaborate, gilded domed structure over a cast-iron well-head topped by a golden elephant. The well was built in the 1860s under the orders of the Maharajah of Benares, in commemoration of his friend Edward Reade, who had some decades earlier financed the construction of a well for the benefit of local people in northern India. At the time, the well was much needed by the people of Stoke Row, since their village lies high above the water table. It was dug – by hand – to a depth of 368ft, more than twice the height of Nelson's Column.

By this point we had joined National Cycle Route 5, which we would follow all the way to the end of the ride at Didcot. It's fairly well signed, so navigation is a breeze; this is particularly handy for anyone keen to stop at the three excellent pubs on this part of route. On the fast freewheel

5m / 5km

down towards Ipsden the western Thames Valley was laid before us in a spectacular vista, and we stopped to enjoy the view at the King William IV at Hailey. After what seemed like ages on quiet country lanes we were back onto busier roads where we crossed the Thames again at Wallingford, though only until the turn into the absurdly attractive village of Brightwell-cum-Sotwell.

From here, the lane rises towards Wittenham Clumps, a distinctive pair of hills topped by beech trees. They once supported late Bronze Age and Iron Age hill forts commanding the Thames valley below; the Romans built on the hills too, and founded the town of Dorchester on Thames, just over the river. It's worth leaving the bikes at the bottom and climbing the Clumps on foot, for they offer impressive views, from the cooling towers of the power station at Didcot to the south-west, right around to the squat tower of Dorchester Abbey to the north-east. The Clumps were the landscape muse of the 20th-century British painter Paul Nash, and the rock group Radiohead, who hail from nearby Abingdon, performed in a sunset webcast from the summit. I've slept the night up there, and the views at sunset were rivalled only by those at sunrise.

The final couple of miles from Long Wittenham were along an excellent off-road cycle track. The Didcot cooling towers looming ahead of us were a reminder of our imminent re-entry into the modern world after a leisurely day enjoying the fun of messing about on the river.

Download route info at thebikeshow.net/17TM

PUBS & PIT STOPS

TEA GARDEN at Sonning Lock RG4 0UR (0118 969 3992) Run in aid of the local air ambulance service, it's a perfect place to stop for a morning coffee and a slice of cake and they also serve cream teas, soft drinks and ice cream.

THE UNICORN Colmore Lane, Kingwood RG9 5LX (01491 628674) Friendly country pub that does food. Half way up the climb to Stoke Row, so a good spot for a breather if required.

KING WILLIAM IV Hailey OX10 6AD (01491 681845) A peach of a country pub, and its terrace is perfectly placed for a sundowner.

THE BLACK HORSE Checkendon RG8 0TE (01491 680418) Run by the same family for over a century. It's quite a time-warp, in a good way. Local ales are tapped from the cask and the only foods served are filled rolls and pickled eggs.

THE RED LION Brightwell-cum-Sotwell OX10 0RT (01491 837373) On summer days, the last of the evening light falls on the drinkers on the small terrace outside this thatched pub. There's beer from Appleford Brewery in the village: it doesn't get any more local than that.

BIKE SHOPS: Action Bikes, 15 West Street, Reading RG1 1TT (0118 951 1345); Henley Cycles, 69 Reading Rd, Henley-on-Thames RG9 1AX (01491 578984); Rides on Air, 11 St Martin Street, Wallingford, Oxfordshire OX10 0AL (01491 836289)

King William IV, Hailey

RIVER TO RIDGEWAY

A round trip heading up the Thames from Reading to a perfect countryside pub set high on the Berkshire Downs

———

There are a handful of days each year when it feels as though the summer will last forever. On these days it's almost impossible to bring to mind the harsh, squally showers of early spring or the mellow scents of autumn, still less the cold, dark afternoons of midwinter. On one of those summer days I rode down the hill from Reading station towards the Thames, where I met two friends for a ride along the river, starting on the Thames Path.

Crossing the river at Caversham Bridge, we ducked into the back lanes. Almost instantly the traffic of Reading had disappeared and we were cruising along through woods and farm fields. The heat of the day was still a few hours away, yet cattle were already sheltering from the sun under huge, spreading oak trees.

Up ahead was Mapledurham House, a stately home in the grand Elizabethan style. It is one of two historic homes that are said to have provided the inspiration for E.H. Shepard's illustrations of Toad Hall in the *Wind in the Willows* stories (*see* Rides No. 7 and No. 8 for more Shepard country). The estate covers much of the surrounding land and most of the small village next to the house. There has been a watermill on the site since at least the time of the Domesday Book, and the current incarnation, which dates back to the 15th century, is the last operational watermill on the Thames. House and mill are open at weekends during the summer (£) and eagle-eyed album cover aficionados will recognise the building from the cover of Ozzy Osbourne's band Black Sabbath's debut LP, where it is depicted with a sinister cloaked figure standing in the foreground. There was nothing of the occult to be seen as we stopped to take in the scene, just the small congregation spilling out into the churchyard across the way from the mill after their morning service.

Heavy rain earlier in the summer ensured the verges of the bridleway were still lush, and the speckled purple spires of marsh orchids stood tall among the grasses at the edge of the track. Between Mapledurham and Whitchurch-on-Thames we passed the other home that may have a claim to being Toad Hall. Hardwick House, a private home, is sadly hidden from this side; from the path on the other side of the river it can be seen, framed by trees.

At Whitchurch we nipped across the Thames to Pangbourne to gather picnic supplies before continuing along a long woodland track on the eastern bank. At this point the river is cutting its way through major hills on both banks: the Chilterns on one side and the Berkshire Downs on the other. It's the closest the Thames ever comes to a gorge, but there are plenty of places from where it's a very easy scramble down to the water's edge.

START & FINISH: Reading, Berkshire • DISTANCE: 30 miles/48km • TOTAL ASCENT: 339m • TERRAIN: Mostly lanes; a few sections of mostly smooth off-road track that could be muddy after heavy rain. Moderate.

Whitchurch-on-Thames

On a hot summer's day there's nothing better than a quick dip, and we ventured gingerly into a Thames that was running fast and high. With a river in spate it's best to take care: we didn't want to risk being swept downstream back to Pangbourne. As we ate our picnic lunch at the foot of a beech tree, looking out at the occasional river boat going by, I made a mental note that this stretch would make a perfect place for an overnight camping trip.

Refreshed and refuelled we rolled on to the Thameside twin villages of Goring and Streatley, at from where we turned our back on the river and began the first real climb of the day, up towards Aldworth. There is a B-road that makes the journey directly, but we opted for a quieter, more scenic alternative: a long lane that peters out into a wide, unsurfaced chalk track. It was dusty and potholed in places but totally passable. This lane forms part of the Ridgeway, an ancient track that most likely began as a drovers' road but went on to serve as a reliable Bronze Age trading route between the Dorset coast and the North Sea in Lincolnshire.

The Ridgeway is now maintained as an 87-mile path open to walkers, horse-riders and cyclists. It runs from the Iron Age hill fort at Ivinghoe Beacon (*see* Ride No. 16) to Avebury, site of the largest Neolithic stone circle in Europe.

Having attained the crest of the Ridgeway we were rewarded with an entirely new landscape laid out before us. Gone was the gentle, fertile valley of the Thames, with its lush green fields and shady woodlands. The soil up here on the Downs is much poorer, and the verges are filled with colourful wildflowers. The harsh conditions and lack of nutrients here mean they can hold their own against the hungry, marauding grasses. The track was lined with delicate, bright red poppies, light-blue pincushion scabious, pinky white studs of achillea, purple tufts of knapweed and sprays of of unidentifiable umbellifers shooting up towards the sky.

By now the sun was really cooking the earth and reflecting bright light off the chalk of the Ridgeway. It was time for the pub, so we headed for the Bell

and slowly sank a couple of pints in the garden as we waited for the baking afternoon to fade into a milder early evening. The Bell is a time warp of a country pub. It has been in the same family for five generations, and in the evenings and on cold days the wood-panelled walls, low-beamed ceiling and huge inglenook fireplace make for a very special atmosphere. There's a serving hatch instead of a bar, and the food is simple but good: crusty bread rolls with a choice of fillings.

Opposite the pub is a well that's said to be the deepest in England. Dug after an outbreak of typhoid in 1868, it reaches 372ft down through solid chalk. It's housed in an impressive tiled building but has been essentially ornamental ever since the village was connected to the mains water supply. In the parish church lie the 'Aldworth Giants': medieval stone effigies of a prominent family from the village. It's impossible to leave a place like Aldworth without promising yourself a return visit before too long.

Fortunately, any sadness at parting was alleviated by the downhill run along high-hedged lanes to cross the River Pang at Tidmarsh. Riding east, I looked over my shoulder and saw the silhouettes of my friends, backlit by the setting sun, riding through the clouds of dust thrown up by our tyres and of pollen drifting down from the trees. The sun had mellowed and everything around us was cast in a soft, golden light.

Suddenly arriving in the western edge of Reading, the roads became busier and it required a careful route-finding to negotiate our way around Tilehurst and onto the traffic-free Thames Path for the last part of the journey back into Reading. As night fell, coloured lights glistered on the wide, black surface of the river. A long hot summer's day had reached its end, just as surely as this seemingly endless summer would, one day, be over.

Download route info at thebikeshow.net/18RR

PUBS & PIT STOPS

THE FERRYBOAT INN High Street, Whitchurch-on-Thames RG8 7DB (0118 984 2161) Relaxed, 18th-century inn with an emphasis on dining.

GREY'S CHEESE COMPANY 17 Reading Road, Pangbourne RG8 7LU (0118 984 3323) Delicatessen specialising in cheese; serves top-notch sandwiches.

LOU LA BELLE 3–5 Reading Rd, Pangbourne RG8 7LR (0118 984 2246) Bright, airy independent café offering a good selection of cakes, sandwiches and hot food.

THE BELL INN Aldworth RG8 9SE (01635 578272) There's no better pub in Britain.

THE GREYHOUND Tidmarsh RG8 8ER (0118 984 3557) Tiny pub with a thatched roof recently restored after being gutted by fire.

BIKE SHOPS: Action Bikes, 15 West Street, Reading RG1 1TT (0118 951 1345); Mountain Mania Cycles, 10 High Street, Goring RG8 9AT (01491 871721)

No.19

A COTSWOLD GETAWAY

From pretty cottages to a megalithic circle, and high culture to tourist traps,
the Cotswolds are a stunning destination for a leisurely weekend
or one long day in the saddle

———

A ride starting just west of Oxford and heading through the Cotswolds might conjure images of dreaming spires and quaint teashops in picturesque villages. It might sound just a bit too chocolate-box. But the Cotswolds I was looking for may have been cycled by Edward Elgar, said to have ridden every lane within 20 miles of his home and many beyond, and were the eponymous subject of the first orchestral symphony by Gustav Holst, also a pioneering cyclist. In poetry, this is the countryside where Burnt Norton provides the anchor for T.S. Eliot's reflections on eternity and salvation, and where time stands still in a vanished railway station. For romantics or historians, stone warriors stand frozen on a hilltop.

I'd normally be inclined to spread a ride like this over two days, either camping wild or splashing out on a plush B&B at the halfway point. But I was riding with an old friend who is a born-again cyclist. As a self-confessed MAMIL (middle aged man in Lycra) he was keen to get in the miles on a single day.

Bicycles are as much a part of the Oxford scene centre as billowing black gowns and punts on the river, and the city is surrounded by some lovely cycling country. Unfortunately, getting out of the city and into the country can be difficult without either a long and tortuous towpath route or a soulless slog alongside a noisy dual carriageway. We were heading for the Cotswolds, so it made sense to stay on the train for one more stop.

Hanborough railway station is home to a pair of small museums (£) that document Oxford's incongruous heyday as a major hub of the British motor industry, the Detroit of the Thames Valley. It all began in the bicycle boom of the 1890s when the 16-year-old William Morris set up a shop repairing bikes at his family's home in Oxford. The business grew, and Morris branched out into motorcycles and cars. After the first world war Morris was the first to introduce Henry Ford's assembly-line approach to manufacturing, and his auto empire grew steadily, as more people could afford cars and the costs of making them kept falling. Morris made a fortune from his vast factories at Cowley and donated most of it to charity. In his youth, he was a champion bike racer, who held seven local records and met his future wife while out cycling. Many of the quiet lanes around these parts are almost unchanged despite the years that have passed since then.

Our route threaded its way up the river Glyme, passing a series of large estates: Blenheim can be visited (£); Glympton Park, Kiddington Hall and Heythrop Park are emphatically private. The quiet, gently rolling lanes were folded in

START & FINISH: Long Hanborough, Oxfordshire • DISTANCE: 66 miles/106km • TOTAL ASCENT: 1124m
TERRAIN: Quiet lanes, with two stretches of A-road with cycle lanes. Challenging in a day, moderate over two.

Rollright Stones

among large fields of ripe wheat and the occasional wooded copse. The biggest landmarks were lone oak trees, towering sentinels in the long lines of hedgerows that divide one field from the next.

Beyond Church Enstone we began a steady climb up to the ridge where Oxfordshire, Warwickshire and Gloucestershire meet. The view from the top is phenomenal, and the ridge must once have been part of a larger sacred landscape, as it is marked not just by burial mounds but also by a trio of Neolithic and Bronze Age monuments, known collectively as the Rollright Stones.

There is no shortage of legends and superstitions surrounding the stones, from medieval times onwards. The King's Men is a wide circle of 77 irregularly shaped stones that resemble a giant gap-toothed mouth. A little way away is the smaller, fenced group of Whispering Knights, and across the road in Warwickshire sits the King Stone, more than two metres high but also somewhat brutally caged in by a metal fence. Its odd, sinuous shape was not the work not of its

prehistoric builders but of much later tourists chipping off souvenirs. The stones featured in a 'Doctor Who' story called *The Stones of Blood*, which I vividly remember watching in a state of terror as a young child, more-or-less from behind the sofa.

The stones are cut from the local oolite, a limestone that was laid down across central England during the Jurassic era, when area of land that is now England was situated much further south, under shallow subtropical seas. The stone is composed of the remains of marine creatures, crushed under pressure over millions of years. Geologically, it is nearly twice as old as the chalk of the Chilterns and the Downs further east. Unlike chalk, oolite is an outstanding building material and its smooth texture and honeyed tones give the Cotswolds its character, from humble drystone walls to modest village churches and grand manor houses. But it is probably the rough-hewn stone walls and tiled roofs of ordinary Cotswold cottages that are so heart-stoppingly beautiful, even if they

have adorned a thousand chocolate boxes.

We rolled into Adlestrop, a village made famous by the poem of the same name, recounting an unscheduled stop on a railway line that now no longer exists. The poet Edward Thomas, a great traveller across the English landscape, captured in a few lines the mood of a hot summer's day in 1914, just months before the horrors of trench warfare destroyed forever the gentility of Edwardian Britain. Thomas himself was killed by a shell blast in Arras in 1917, not long after writing the poem. The brown-and-cream station sign still hangs in the village bus shelter.

After crossing the Evenlode river we climbed up the hill to Stow-on-the-Wold, one of a handful of handsome Cotswold towns that treads a pre-carious line between the most attractive in the world and a coach-tour horror show. The acerbic columnist and restaurant critic A.A. Gill described the town as 'catastrophically ghastly'. Certainly, it's a honey-pot brimming with honey, in the form of tea rooms and shops selling antiques, junk and tourist knick-knacks. Yet there's no denying the beauty of Stow's many fine buildings, most of which were built with money earned from wool.

A medieval saying had it that 'in Europe the best wool is English, in England the best wool is Cotswold'. Wool was to the medieval economy what oil is to our industrial age, and the trade was just as international and equally lucrative. Cotswold sheep produced the finest wool and commanded the highest prices. Apparently it was all down to a small, lively breed of sheep that was suited to a life roaming freely over hilly, windswept land, grazing on short, fine grasses. From the shepherds up, there was an entire feudal economy plugged in to a capitalist network of traders and bankers as far away as Antwerp and Florence, which were the centres of medieval cloth-making. Wool was bought and sold on credit, and there were spot prices and forward contracts that suggest medieval wool traders would be perfectly at home trading in today's global commodity markets. They'd probably appreciate exchanging the abacus for the Bloomberg Terminal.

From Stow we rode on to the Slaughters, a pair of villages that embody the beauty of the Cotswolds, untouched by new building for over a century. As they weren't overrun with tourists, we spent a relaxing half hour wandering about, stopping to dip our feet in the waters of the clear-running stream that flows from the Upper to the Lower village.

We rode on through Bourton-on-the-Water but didn't dwell, for the town has definitely crossed to the wrong side of the line as a tourist trap, at least in summer. It was heaving with crowds traipsing after umbrella-wielding tour guides, coaches belching diesel and an overwhelming sense of commercial tawdriness. I made a mental note to return in the dead of winter, when the coach parties are gone – perhaps on a day when the town is cloaked in white after a snowfall.

Continuing south, we joined National Cycle Route 47 at Farmington, where a group of cheerful ducks were waddling about in the road outside the pub: always a good sign of a quiet lanes to come. Sherborne parish church features some exquisite Georgian marble memorials, including a dramatic scene entitled *The Guardian Angel Tramples Death Underfoot*. Opposite is a tablet featuring a highly conspicuous and potentially embarrassing mistake by the stonemason that has been crossed out and corrected.

The Windrush valley was laid out to our left like a pastoral fantasy of the English countryside, the river meandering through meadows grazed by cattle with rich brown coats. On the way out of the village of Little Barrington a strange contraption on a front garden lawn caught my eye. We got talking with the old gent whose house it was and it turned out he was a blacksmith, one of a family

River Windrush

line in the valley, and that the contraption was the old gravity-powered bellows from his forge. When his son took on the business he had upgraded to more modern equipment, but he couldn't bring himself to junk a piece of local history, so there it stands in his front garden.

The valley just got better and better as we whizzed through Burford and across the river at Asthall. The sun was setting behind us, throwing our shadows onto the road ahead. It was early September and many of the fields had already been harvested; the cool, monochrome light of dusk felt like a taste of the winter to come.

We passed the ruins of Minster Lovell Hall, a large house built by William Lovell, one of Richard III's close allies, but forfeited when the Tudors seized the throne after defeating Richard at the Battle of Bosworth Field. The house was subsequently owned by two of Henry VIII's

'grooms of the stool', powerful courtiers whose tasks ranged from the magnificent (overseeing the royal finances) to the menial (literally, wiping the king's bum). It was abandoned in the 18th century and its ruins are now cared for by English Heritage. It made for an eerie spot as night was creeping all around us.

After a long day in the saddle I was now feeling every mile. It was a relief to finish the final climb, out of the Windrush Valley. The last stretch was an unavoidable slog along the main road into Long Hanborough. I was all in. It'd been a terrific day's ride, through some of southern England's most treasured landscape and most photographed villages. By bicycle, we'd managed to escape the crowds and find our own version of the Cotswolds, every bit a match for Elgar's, Holst's or Eliot's.

Download route info at thebikeshow.net/19CG

PUBS & PIT STOPS

CROWN INN Mill Lane, Church Enstone OX7 4NN (01608 677262) Pleasant village pub.

THE FOX INN The Green, Broadwell GL56 0UF (01451 870909) Handsome Cotswold village pub serving beer from the nearby Donnington Brewery.

NORTH'S COTSWOLD BAKERY Church Street, Stow-on-the-Wold GL54 1BE (01451 870720) Top notch flapjacks and other temptations.

THE TALBOT The Square, Stow-on-the-Wold GL54 1BQ (01451 870934) Relaxed pub/restaurant that prides itself on home cooking.

HAMPTONS FINEFOODS 1 Digbeth Street, Stow-on-the-Wold GL54 1BN (01451 831733)

LORDS OF THE MANOR Upper Slaughter GL54 2JD (01451 820243) Lighten the wallet in fine style at a hotel with a Michelin-starred restaurant.

MOORS FARM CAMPSITE Moor Lane, Bourton-on-the-Water GL54 2HA (01451 821030). A handful of pitches in tranquil surroundings on a working farm, open March–October.

THE FOX INN Little Barrington OX18 4TB (01451 844385) Idyllic location, very comfortable rooms for overnight stays.

BURFORD offers plenty of choice.

BIKE SHOPS: Bourton Cycles, Bourton Industrial Park, Bourton-on-the-Water GL54 2HQ (01451 822323)

HERTS,
BEDS & BUCKS

CHILTERN RENDEZVOUS

A ride out from Hertfordshire into Buckinghamshire to the Ivinghoe Beacon, the most prominent summit in the Chilterns, returning through the Ashridge Estate

——

The Chilterns are a range of chalk hills that stretch about 45 miles diagonally from Luton in the north-east to the River Thames at Goring in the south-west, dotted with Neolithic and Iron Age forts and burial mounds. The hills also mark the southern limit of the Scandinavian ice sheet that covered most of Britain and Ireland some half a million years ago. Back then it was a hostile, lifeless environment – one that my teenage friends and I had unwittingly managed to experience for ourselves on a frozen winter night many years ago.

Six of us had decided that February was a good time to cycle out to camp on Ivinghoe Beacon, one of the highest points in the Chilterns. Heavy rain soaked us and our gear on the ride out. Then when night fell, it started snowing. One of the tents had a large hole in the groundsheet. The camping gas wouldn't light. Only foolish 15-year-olds would attempt to get warm by stripping naked and running energetically up the hill: it didn't work. I remember eating cold tinned ravioli and shivering, while a gale-force wind howled around us. That night taught me lot about how not to camp.

I had planned a ride to revisit the site of my teenage camping disaster, so there I was with a cup of tea and round of toast and Marmite from a little kiosk outside Harpenden station, waiting for a cycling journalist friend, who lives nearby, to

meet me. It was mid August and he was back from covering the Tour de France and the Olympics. As we rolled down Harpenden's broad high street, he confessed to feeling out of shape after six weeks of cheap hotels, bad food and hard work. He was astride a carbon-fibre road bike, dressed head-to-foot in lycra and in the mood for getting in the miles.

The slopes of the Chilterns are very gradual on the eastern approach, much steeper on the western side, and as we rode west up the shallow slope of the escarpment, the upward gradient was almost imperceptible. We reached the ridge at Whipsnade, home to a countryside outpost of London Zoo and Europe's first 'safari park', where animals are not confined to pens and cages (£). It opened in 1931 with exotic birds, deer and skunks; today it pulls the crowds with a menagerie that includes lions, rhinos, cheetahs, a small herd of Asian elephants, bears, penguins and moose. Over the road from the zoo is the Whipsnade Tree Cathedral, a 10-acre garden of trees and shrubs planted in the approximate shape of a cathedral in an act of 'faith, hope and reconciliation' after the horrors of the first world war. It's free to visit.

We stopped just beyond Whipsnade for the fine view westwards across the Vale of Aylesbury from the top of Bison Hill. We could see Ivinghoe

---

START & FINISH: Harpenden, Hertfordshire • DISTANCE: 43 miles/70km • TOTAL ASCENT: 507m
TERRAIN: Quiet lanes, a couple of short sections on main roads. Moderate.

Ashridge Estate

Beacon to the south, and as we flew down the hill I was conscious that all this altitude we were losing would eventually have to be regained – but not before a pleasant spin on the lanes through Eaton Bray and Slapton towards Mentmore.

Shortly before Mentmore, after leaving the B488, we rode under the railway line at Bridego Bridge, site of the infamous 1963 Great Train Robbery. It remains one of the biggest robberies in British history, and the bulk of the £2.6 million (£41 million in today's money) was never recovered. Three of the culprits were never caught and two of those that were convicted escaped prison. One of them, Ronnie Biggs, fled to Brazil and lived the life of a celebrity villain for decades before returning to the United Kingdom voluntarily, saying he wanted to 'walk into a Margate pub as an Englishman and buy a pint of bitter'.

From here we turned back south to Mentmore, a small village of impressive red-brick houses. In the centre of the village we passed the elaborate and firmly closed wrought-iron gates of Mentmore

Towers. This huge, elaborate 'Jacobethan' country house was built in the 1850s for the banker Baron Mayer de Rothschild, and designed to house one of the finest collections of art and furniture in the country: the closest Britain came to the Hermitage in Russia. The house and collection were offered to the state in lieu of death duties in the 1970s, but the government rejected it. The family sold much of the collection and the house was bought for £220,000 by the Transcendental Meditation movement founded by Maharishi Mahesh Yogi, guru to the Beatles. It subsequently served as the headquarters of the movement's political arm, the Natural Law Party, whose 1992 election manifesto included a commitment to make yogic flying a core principle of the National Health Service. The estate was then sold to a property developer whose plans to turn it into a hotel ran into financial trouble; it has had more success in the movies, appearing as Wayne Mansions in *Batman Begins* and in other films from *Ali G Indahouse* to *The Mummy Returns*. But the roof of the house is

5m / 8km

leaking, and Mentmore now appears on English Heritage's 'at risk' list.

Riding onwards, we crossed over the Grand Union Canal and then the railway line and into Ivinghoe, with the Beacon coming clearly into view up ahead. On this summer's day it looked entirely benign, but memories of shivering in a wet sleeping bag on that awful February night still sent a shiver down my spine.

The hills of the Chilterns are so weathered that it's difficult to speak of summits in the traditional sense. Though not the highest point, Ivinghoe Beacon is the most prominent 'top' in the range. The road up is a regular testing ground for hill-climbing cyclists and has featured in plenty of races, from local cyclosportives to the Tour of Britain. The Beacon is also the meeting point of the Icknield Way, which runs north-east towards Norfolk (*see* Ride No. 21) and the Ridgeway, which heads south-west towards Avebury (*see* Ride No. 18). The climb isn't especially steep but it is long, and I soon raced ahead of my lycra-clad friend, who was muttering something about having been too long out of the saddle and eaten too much rich food on *Le Tour*. Regrouping at the top, we rode through the Ashridge Estate, a haven for walkers and mountain-bikers that is criss-crossed with fantastic tracks through the mature, broad-leafed forests. Two short, sharp climbs brought us to Gaddesden Row, and by then we were on the home stretch.

After a very good espresso in the sunshine at The Hub, Redbourn's own cycling cafe, I rolled slowly along the lanes back to Harpenden; there is a rougher, traffic-free alternative from Redbourn along the Nickey Line, a disused railway line converted to a cycling and walking path. My route included one last and unexpected hill, bringing my total climbing for the day to just over 650m. By no means alpine, but I felt as though I'd seen the best of the hills of this north-eastern edge of the Chilterns and, as a bonus, had exorcised my teenage memories of that freezing night on a bare mountain.

Download route info at thebikeshow.net/20CR

PUBS & PIT STOPS

THE CARPENTERS ARMS 1 Horton Road, Slapton LU7 9DB (01525 220563) Historic, thatch-roofed pub.

THE ROSE AND CROWN Vicarage Lane, Ivinghoe LU7 9EQ (01296 668472) Cosy pub serving real ales and hearty food.

THE BRIDGEWATER ARMS Little Gaddesden HP4 1PD (01442 842408) Well-placed pub with a large garden and good value food.

OLD CHEQUERS Gaddesden Row, Hemel Hempstead HP2 6HH (01442 256315) Oak-beamed country pub with an emphasis on dining.

THE ALFORD ARMS Frithsden HP1 3DD (01422 864480) Slightly off the route, an upmarket dining pub with sunny terrace.

THE HUB 22 High Street, Redbourn AL3 7LL (01582 792389) Top-quality coffee and cake at Redbourn's cycling cafe. Also bicycle repair and cycle hire.

BIKE SHOP: Harpenden Cycles, 115a Southdown Road, Harpenden AL5 1QQ (01582 461963)

BIKE HIRE: The Hub (see listing above)

SPECIALIST TEAS

BIKE & BODY BOOST

CYCLE · SPOR

WELL DONE WIGGO

The Hub, Redbourn

No.21

HIDDEN HERTFORDSHIRE

A quiet corner of the home counties that's full of unexpected delights,
from an Iron Age hill fort to a haunted chapel.

———

The playwright, philosopher and wit George Bernard Shaw took up cycling at the relatively late age of 29, when the first chain-driven safety bicycles appeared, but he was an enthusiastic convert. Rather than take lessons, he taught himself and crashed a lot, causing him to reflect that he might have suffered less had he taken up boxing. On holiday in Monmouthshire in 1895 with philosopher Bertrand Russell, he rear-ended his cycling companion, completely wrecking the young philosopher's bicycle while Shaw suffered not so much as a scratch. Forced to take the train home, Russell had to endure taunting by the athletic Shaw, who managed to keep up with the train on his bicycle and stopped at every station just to prove the point.

At the height of his literary fame, Shaw moved to Ayot St Lawrence in rural Hertfordshire. Could it be that he was drawn to this quiet, charming little pocket of England because it is such good cycling country? That's what I set out to discover. For added literary clout, I planned my ride to trace, in a roundabout way, the catchment around the start of the river Mimram, a tributary of the River Lea and the subject of Stevie Smith's poem *River God*.

I began my journey at Knebworth, and rode up the quiet country lane past Knebworth House, which lives a double life as both an elegant stately home and, since 1974, a venue for some of the biggest outdoor concerts in the country. Acts like Led Zeppelin, Deep Purple, Queen, Oasis and more recently the Red Hot Chili Peppers have drawn huge crowds, and generated long traffic jams on the nearby A1. Such scenes were hard to imagine as I rolled along in the morning sunshine, wheat fields swaying in the warm breeze, on lanes quite deserted of all traffic but for the occasional farm vehicle.

It was a short climb up to Ayot St Lawrence, and on arriving I leant my bike up by the Brocket Arms and wandered over to the old parish church, which is now a ruin. It stands magnificently in a peaceful, wooded glade with a few tombstones lining the path from the road. Shaw's house in the village, a quite newly built Edwardian villa which he renamed 'Shaw's Corner' (£), is now owned by the National Trust. Its Arts and Crafts interiors and 1930s furniture, complete with indoor exercise bike, are preserved as they were when he died. So too is his tiny, rotating wooden writing hut, complete with typewriter, telephone and wicker chair.

The next 7 miles were an undulating ascent as far as Breachwood Green, a small village that's just a mile from the runway at Luton Airport, directly

---

START & FINISH: Knebworth, Hertfordshire • DISTANCE: 37 miles/60km • TOTAL ASCENT: 586m
TERRAIN: Quiet country lanes, short bridleway to reach ruined chapel. Moderate.

Ayot St Lawrence

on the flight path, and whose blighted residents have led the campaign against any expansion of the airport. From here it would be possible to make a short-cut through Kings Walden and shave 13 miles from the ride, but I was keen to make it to the head of the valley at Deacon Hill, for the view from the summit out across the plains of Bedfordshire. As I rode the bridge across the busy A505 I looked down and watched a lone cyclist in a high-vis tabard, doggedly battling up the dual carriageway as trucks and cars roared past him.

The A505 shadows the route of the Icknield Way, a prehistoric trackway that runs diagonally across most of southern England, south-west to north-east. A little way to the north of the road, after Lilley, I came to the real Icknield Way, an unsurfaced path that for much of its length is open to cyclists. It was summer and the ground was dry, so I couldn't resist riding a short section of this ancient way, as far as Deacon Hill. The alternative, sticking to the road via Hexton and Pegsdon (as shown on the map), is a little longer but probably faster and certainly easier riding. The bridleway was passable but on my touring bike it was hard going, rough and overgrown in parts. I was convinced I'd get a puncture, or end up, like George Bernard Shaw, upside-down in a bed of nettles. One section was so steep I had to walk, and was immediately followed by a white-knuckle descent that I rode hanging onto the brake levers. Of course, had I been on a mountain bike with fat tyres and suspension, it would have been a breeze.

After that excitement, I left my bike at the foot of Deacon Hill and walked up to the top, where it's easy to make out the lumpy remains of an Iron Age hill fort. Sitting at the top and eating my lunch, the view I had come for was breathtaking: a patchwork of golden fields and pasture rolling away to the horizon. It would make for a superb overnight bivvy spot, though English Nature,

which manages the land here, would not approve, if they ever found out.

After a morning riding west and north it was time to turn back. I followed a well-marked cycle route along a potholed lane through the quiet, somehow eerie hamlets of Wellbury and Little Offley. After recrossing the A505, again by bridge, I rolled quickly along tranquil lanes past two outstanding country pubs in Ley Green and Preston.

I sped along these lanes, as I was now on a mission to find Minsden Chapel. The ruined remains of a 14th century church in the middle of nowhere make a prime location for ghost stories, and Minsden has plenty to its name. They include a phantom monk, eerie music hanging in the air around the chapel and bells tolling in the middle of the night. The ghosts of a murdered nun and a small child are said to haunt the grounds, and there are legends of secret tunnels leading away from the chapel and treasure buried by the Knights Templar, who had their English headquarters in the county. With all these myths and

legends, I was keen to take a look. The flint walls are still standing even as they are gradually being swallowed up by the undergrowth. It's a peaceful, atmospheric spot, but I saw no ghosts and heard nothing but birdsong and the wind in the trees that lean over and threaten to enclose the ruins.

After the disappointment of finding no paranormal activity whatsoever, I consoled myself with a cup of tea and a slice of homemade cake at the ever-popular Emily's Tea Shop in Whitwell. More than just a tea shop, Emily's is part of a small open farm with pigs, goats, sheep, hens and ducks. There are horses too, and a little bicycle repair workshop. Whitwell is a fine village of 18th century brick and half-timbered houses. The source of the Mimram is just west of the village here, and it's a far cry from the sinister, smelly deity of Smith's poem. Nine Wells Farm, as its name suggests, draws clean water from limestone aquifers deep underground, and this has been a local centre of watercress production for two centuries. There are two watercress harvests a year: from March to May and from September to December.

Watercress is rich in iron, calcium, folic acid and vitamins A and C, and is also said to be a stimulant, an antioxidant and protective against cancer. George Bernard Shaw was a lifelong vegetarian, and I'm sure he ate his fair share of watercress from the beds of the Mimram. He died in his garden, aged 94, after falling off a ladder while pruning an apple tree. With his long life in mind, I bought a small bag, tucked it into my pannier and rode the short climb back up to Knebworth to catch the train home.

Download route info at thebikeshow.net/21HH

PUBS & PIT STOPS

THE BROCKET ARMS Ayot St Lawrence AL6 9BT (01438 820250) Cosy, historic oak-beamed inn, with rooms for overnight stays.

THE RED LION Great Offley SG5 3DZ (01462 768281) Decent village pub with a reputation for good food.

THE PLOUGH Plough Lane, Preston SG4 8LA (01438 871394) No-frills village pub serving basic bar food and homemade specials.

THE RED LION Preston SG4 7UD (01462 459585) Britain's first community-owned pub. Real ales and excellent food.

THE STRATHMORE ARMS St Paul's Walden SG4 8BT (01438 871654) Traditional, unspoilt drinker's pub serving simple food.

EMILY'S TEA SHOP Water Hall Farm, Whitwell SG4 8BN (0143887 1928) Near-legendary cyclists' tea stop serving home made cakes.

Deacon Hill

No.22

FARMLAND FANTASTIC

A gentle ride on the lanes of eastern Bedfordshire, through the arable fields
and historic villages of the Ivel Valley to a stunning nature reserve,
home to Europe's largest wildlife conservation charity

———

The market town of Baldock grew up at the junction of the ancient drovers' route of Icknield Way and the Great North Road coaching road. The transformation of the latter into the impassable A1 has saved Baldock and its pretty medieval centre from being swallowed up by the larger and younger Letchworth Garden City, the first of the 'new towns', founded just over a century ago. Sitting at such an important travellers' crossroad may account for Baldock having a large number of pubs for a town of its size – or perhaps they opened to serve drinkers from Letchworth, a 'dry' city for the first 50 years of its existence.

Baldock station is on the very northern outskirts of the town, and within minutes we were into the open fields and big skies of the Bedfordshire–Hertfordshire border. This is prime arable country, and there are few trees or hedgerows to break up the landscape. But the land is gently rolling and not boringly flat, which makes for good cycling. It is also where East Anglia begins and most of the rivers in the area flow north through the prairies of Cambridgeshire and empty into the North Sea at the Wash.

The first place we came to was Ashwell, an exceptionally handsome village with its own museum maintained by local enthusiasts. It has a collection of maps, photographs and artefacts that tell the everyday story of this village over the centuries and also speak of the history of so many others in Britain. For years the Ashwell village post was delivered on a bike by Flo Worboys, who worked well into her eighties and was eventually awarded the OBE. The museum has a charming black and white photograph of Flo wearing a beret and winged glasses and holding her post-bike, a banana box mounted on the front and stuffed with letters.

The imposing tower of Ashwell's 14th century church is visible from quite a way away, but what I was most interested to see was some unusual medieval graffiti, in a mixture of Latin and early English, carved on the stone walls inside. One wall tells of how a 'pitiable, fierce, violent plague' afflicted the 'wretched populace' in 1350. The pillars feature proverbs and some more light-hearted scrawls, including 'The Archdeacon is an ass', 'Barbara is a regular young vixen' and an architect's disapproving comment on the construction of the building, 'the corners are not jointed correctly. I spit on them.'

These lands were among the first in Britain to be cleared of their native woodland by early Neolithic farmers, who started by domesticating livestock and then planted cereals and other crops. Farming has remained an important part of life

---

START & FINISH: Baldock, Hertfordshire • DISTANCE: 35 miles/56km • TOTAL ASCENT: 195m
TERRAIN: Mostly lanes, quieter B-roads and two short sections of off-road path. Moderate.

The Cock. Broom

here ever since, and changes in agriculture have shaped both the landscape and the plants and animals that live on farmed land.

In the late 19th century, a local man named Dan Albone, who was a successful racing cyclist, engineer and entrepreneur, invented Britain's first commercially successful farm tractor. Whatever went before, none of the changes can have been more rapid and profound than those of the past half-century. Increased mechanisation, new breeds of crops and new artificial fertilisers have changed farming practices beyond recognition. Herbicides and pesticides have eradicated many traditional wildflowers and insects, and farmland birds like the lapwing, linnet and skylark are far fewer in number. Thinking about it, as we cruised north along narrow lanes through golden fields, under a blue sky dotted with puffy clouds, we were conscious of how quiet it was. There was very little birdsong. Looking into a field of wheat there was nothing to see but the crop's stocky stalks and the hard, grey-brown soil.

The road turns uphill into the town of Potton, which sits on the eastern slope of a diagonal ridge of sandstone, and continues to climb to the village of Everton. Here we noticed a distinct change in the landscape – suddenly it was more wooded, and there was heather and gorse around.

We took a turn down a forest track to reach the headquarters of the Royal Society for the Protection of Birds (RSPB), a country house set in 180 acres of woodland, heath and meadow. For more than two decades the RSPB has led the campaign to moderate the impact of modern agriculture on the environment and to restore important habitats as refuges for birds, insects and native plants. It walks the talk too, farming in an environmentally responsible way on a 450-acre arable farm a few miles over the border in Cambridgeshire. In the past ten years Hope Farm has bucked the national downward trend in farmland bird populations

while still turning a commercial profit, showing that modern productivity needn't come at the expense of wildlife. The RSPB encourages cycling on many of its nature reserves, and we followed a track through beautiful broadleaf woodland to come out on the smooth, traffic-free cycle route across Biggleswade common, the largest expanse of common land in Bedfordshire.

Skirting around Biggleswade we headed for The Cock Inn at Broom, a country pub with what might seem like an insurmountable problem: it has no bar. Not even a serving hatch. Instead, there is a doorway into a subterranean tap room. I placed our orders at the doorway, and the drinks were handed up to me. We sat in one of the pub's

five cosy, wood-panelled rooms, while a clattering game of bar skittles was going on next door.

Our earlier dawdling at the RSPB's nature reserve meant it was late afternoon by the time we hit the road again, with 15 miles still to go. This was not a route that leaves the best until last, so we put our heads down and rode quickly through the suburban village of Langford, crossing the A1 by a bridge. From there, the quiet country lanes and a final short climb took us through Hinxworth and back up to Ashwell, a village that's worth at least a second visit, before retracing our tracks to Baldock.

Download route info at thebikeshow.net/22FF

PUBS & PIT STOPS

THE BUSHEL & STRIKE 15 Mill Street, Ashwell SG7 5LY (01462 742394) Opposite the church, a pub with a popular restaurant attached.

THE ROSE & CROWN 69 High Street, Ashwell SG7 5NP (01462 742394) Friendly village pub with seasonally changing food menu.

THE JOHN O'GAUNT INN Sutton SG19 2NE (01767 260377) Small country pub serving homemade food. Garden outside and open fires in winter.

THE COACH HOUSE 12 Market Square, Potton SG19 2NP (01767 260221) Has had an upmarket makeover and serves a menu of locally-sourced food with rooms for overnight stays.

POTTON is a good place to buy picnic supplies, and there are also several other pubs in the town offering traditional pub fare.

THE COCK 23 High Street, Broom SG18 9NA (01767 314411) Extraordinary rural pub with no bar. Good beers and honest pub food.

THE THREE HORSESHOES High Street, Hinxworth SG7 5HQ (01462 742280) Village pub with a thatched roof. Serves food and afternoon teas.

BIKE SHOPS: Pedals, 20 Back Street, Biggleswade SG18 8JA (01767 313418); Byercycles, 16 Shefford Road, Clifton SG17 5RG (01462 811175).

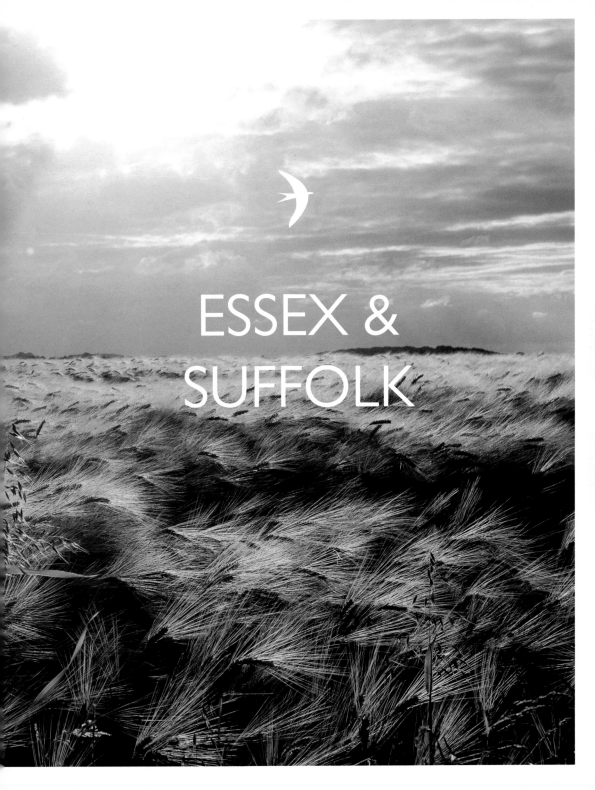

ESSEX & SUFFOLK

EMPTY ESSEX

A flat landscape might seem uninspiring, but the wild Dengie marshes are southern England's big-sky country and steeped in history

---

Southminster sits sleepily at the very end of a single-track branch line that creeps out to the pancake-flat marshes of the eastern Dengie peninsula. It's a lonesome place, and as we rode out towards the sea the roads were as empty as the landscape. There were no hedgerows and few trees, just vast, open fields, towering stacks of straw bales and menacing tractors lurking in farmyards, baring ferocious metal talons of every size and shape. The deep blue sky was criss-crossed by aircraft vapour trails and delicate wisps of high cloud. Was this Essex, or Nebraska?

It's hard to imagine amid the emptiness, but archaeologists have found that these marshes have been occupied and worked continuously since Neolithic times. The land we were riding on was reclaimed from the sea from the 16th century onwards. The lanes that reach out towards the coast, only to stop apparently in the middle of nowhere, are testament to this process; once, they reached the coast and were used for loading farm produce onto ships for transport by sea.

But it would be naive to think the current situation is the end of the story; the sea still comes back from time to time. In the great North Sea Storm of 1953, which claimed hundreds of lives along Britain's east coast, the flood waters covered hundreds of acres of Dengie farmland. With global sea levels on the rise, it's only a matter of time before the floods come again. Maintaining defences is an expensive business, and the talk is now of 'managed retreat': allowing coastal land to revert to a salt marsh that acts like a sponge, absorbing storm waters and sheltering the remaining inland farm fields from future floods. The Dengie coastal marshes are protected under national and international schemes, and provide a vital habitat for a variety of wetland birds.

Much of the reclamation was done by people living in and around Tillingham, a village whose entry in the Domesday book records a relatively large population of 32 households, 15 cattle, 30 pigs and 340 sheep. The marshes were a good place for grazing sheep and hunting wildfowl, and there were plenty of fish and shellfish to catch in the estuaries.

In the religious upheavals that followed Britain's break with Rome, Tillingham bore witness to the turbulence of the time. The return of Catholicism after the death of Henry VIII was not popular in Essex, and the Protestant local lord of the manor was burned at the stake in Mary Tudor's Catholic purges. During Cromwell's rule, a religious pamphlet against non-conformists told

---

START: Southminster, Essex • FINISH: Burnham-on-Crouch, Essex • DISTANCE: 28 miles/44km
TOTAL ASCENT: 62m • TERRAIN: Quiet country lanes, with a few miles of of smooth, unsurfaced track that may be soft after heavy rain. Easy.

a grisly story of a young woman of the village who, soon after joining a sect known as the Ranters, claimed to have fallen pregnant through immaculate conception. Imprisoned for heresy, she was reported to have borne a dead baby with claws in place of hands and feet, before erupting in boils and scabs and stabbing herself to death.

Tillingham felt altogether more tranquil as we stopped on the village green in front of the 12th-century church to fix a puncture. Harvest time often brings punctures, as farm vehicles spread sharp fragments of flint and other debris from the fields into the lanes. The wait gave us time to take in the scene and have a closer look at the village water pump that still stands on the green opposite the Fox and Hounds pub.

Historically, only the most prestigious buildings, such as the village church, were made of stone, and even those are a mixture of compacted flint and rubble. Lacking a ready source of stone, Essex people made use of wood instead. The walls of the earliest timber-framed buildings were simply filled with wattle and daub but later, to achieve better protection from the elements, they were plastered in decorative patterns or clad with overlapping timber planks. With the advent of cheaper, imported timber in the late 18th century, more buildings could be weatherboarded. The cottages on the green at Tillingham look the part but are actually late-Victorian imitations.

From Tillingham we continued along the lanes to the village of Bradwell-on-Sea, which is in fact a little way inland, and from there we followed a long track to the land's end, where stands one of the oldest Christian buildings in the country, dating back to an even earlier religious tussle. In the 7th and 8th century, Essex, or the Kingdom of the East Saxons, was was converted back and forth between Christianity and paganism. A decisive figure in the eventual triumph of Christianity was a missionary monk named Cedd, who sailed

St Peter's Chapel

down the coast from the monastery at Lindisfarne in Northumberland. St Cedd, as he became after his death, founded many churches in Essex – including the Chapel of St Peter-on-the-Wall here, where he first came ashore.

Fourteen hundred years later the chapel still stands, like a great barn, a stocky, defiant vertical in the flat marshlands. We stepped into its cavernous interior and suddenly it felt very calm. Rays of sunlight played across the rough stone walls of a perfectly proportioned refuge from the big skies and wide-open spaces outside. The chapel is a testament to Cedd's determination, but also owes a debt to the construction skills of the Romans, who had built a fortress here five centuries earlier. Cedd recycled stone from the fort for the chapel's walls, which are some three feet thick, and the solid Roman foundations have prevented the building from being swallowed up by the marsh. Next to the chapel, in a clearing among a grove of trees, is the Othona spiritual community, named after the old Roman fort. It was founded here in 1946, and it still offers a home, retreats and working weeks for people of all backgrounds and beliefs, worshipping in the ancient church.

From the chapel, a track follows the coast north around Sale Point. Looking out to sea, a row of eleven barges beached on the mudflats represents a more recent effort to protect the land from the water. Further around the headland is a series of white-sand beaches at the mouth of the Blackwater estuary – suddenly we were at the classic British seaside. Yachts with bright sails dotted water flecked with white caps of surf, and families larked around on the sand and in the shallows.

I took a dip and found the water to be surprisingly warm for the North Sea. My friends said this must be because of the nuclear power station, two squat grey blocks that crouch on the coast, built to use the seawater for cooling. They were pulling my leg: Bradwell's reactors were turned off ten years ago and the plant is now being dismantled. A new reactor is rumoured; more immediately, two wind farms are under construction on the marshes. With all that flat land it's hardly surprising, but the battle between those who see a natural, clean energy source and those who want to keep the skies big and empty is bringing out a tenacity in the locals that feels as old as Essex itself.

We rode on along the path to Bradwell Waterside, a small lagoon and yachting marina. There's something relaxing about watching people messing about in boats, and we stopped to take in the scene among the ramshackle jumble of jetties, boats and ropes until the likelihood that the pub would be closing its kitchen called us back inland to Bradwell village for lunch.

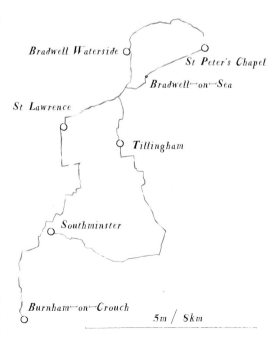

Having devoured a table laden with pub grub's greatest hits – lasagne, scampi, and ham, egg and chips (twice) – we bade farewell to Bradwell and its two iconic, contrasting buildings: the 7th-century temple to the power of the word of God and the 20th-century temple to the power of the atom.

As we rode south, we felt an unusual sensation for the roads of Dengie: a very slight incline. This was confirmed as we approached a water tower at St Lawrence. Water towers and radio transmitters are a reliable indicators of high ground, and passing any of these structures is a sign of having reached the top of a hill. Dengie is so flat that St Lawrence, just 35m above sea level, qualifies as high ground. Still, its concrete water tower, shaped like a Martini glass, is an impressive structure.

Nearby stands a wrought iron beacon, a device that might be seen as a very early version of the radio transmitter. In the Elizabethan era, when Britain feared invasion by the Spanish Armada, a series of coastal warning beacons were established. The idea was that when the Armada was first sighted, a beacon would immediately be set alight. As soon as one beacon was seen, the next one along the coast would be lit, and the message would eventually reach London. Depending on how alert the local people were, and how dry the firewood, the message could have travelled quite quickly.

We rolled gently down from the dizzy heights of St Lawrence, passing through Southminster again and on to Burnham-on-Crouch, an elegant seaside town on the River Crouch. It's popular for yachting, and on summer evenings all the action is down on the long, straight quayside, which is backed by a row of inns, boathouses and houses of all ages and architectural styles. The waters of the Crouch were silky calm and carried the reflection of a sunset sky, all yellows and oranges, in the west. It was a spectacular sight and a fitting end to a day of effortlessly exploring these lonely, forgotten marshlands that hold two millennia of history.

Download route info at thebikeshow.net/23EE

PUBS & PIT STOPS

THE FOX & HOUNDS The Square, Tillingham CM0 7SU (01621 779416) Victorian pub on village green with sunny terrace.

CAP AND FEATHERS 8 South Street, Tillingham CM0 7TJ (01621 779212) Weather-boarded free house, with rooms for overnight stays.

THE KINGS HEAD High Street, Bradwell-on-Sea CM0 7QL (01621 776224) Red-brick village pub, food served at lunchtimes.

THE GREEN MAN Waterside, Bradwell-on-Sea CM0 7QX (01621 776226) Exposed oak beams, whitewashed walls and an open fireplace. Food served, with an emphasis on fish. Rooms for overnight stays.

YE OLDE WHITE HARTE HOTEL The Quay, Burnham-on-Crouch CM0 8AS (01621 782106) One of three quayside pubs, perfect for watching the sunset.

No.24

THE OYSTER RUN

By bike and by boat, a day on the Essex coast in search of the county's prized mollusc,
with a Tiptree cream tea thrown in for good measure

——

When the Romans invaded Britain they brought their cuisine with them, livening up the British diet considerably. They imported dates, almonds, olives and olive oil, wine, pine nuts, pepper, ginger and cinnamon. They also popularised the use of herbs like parsley, mint and rosemary, introduced cabbages and cucumbers, raised game birds like pheasants and guinea fowl and planted fruit trees such as the medlar, mulberry, damson and plum – all so firmly embedded in our food history that it's hard to remember they were not always here.

As a culinary exchange, this was all was incredibly one-sided, except for one British delicacy: the oyster. Native Britons only ate oysters as a last resort, but archaeologists have found enormous piles of oyster shells, sometimes as many as a million, among the remains of Roman forts and villas. And they favoured not just any oyster, but the oyster that grew in the muddy, marshy estuaries of Essex. They even sent Essex oysters back to Rome. The Romans chose Colchester as their capital for strategic and political reasons, but it must have been a happy coincidence that it was close to a plentiful supply of one of their favourite foods, in the Blackwater estuary and around the island of Mersea.

Since then the oyster has come in and out of fashion. In the late 19th century pollution and over-fishing nearly killed the fisheries, but a few held out,

among them the Blackwater. Both the Colchester Natives, which are prized around the world, and rock oysters, originally from the Pacific, are harvested here; there's nothing quite like eating a plateful of the freshest specimens while sitting among the wooden beach shacks and boats that lean lazily on the mudflats at West Mersea.

A dozen of us met at Colchester train station and rode down into the town to join the cycle path that loosely follows the River Colne flowing eastwards towards the sea. At the head of the estuary, Wivenhoe is one of a handful of nautical-arty towns that pepper the British coastline – think of Whitstable, Rye, and Aldeburgh, or further afield, Bridlington and St Ives. Some say it's the quality of the light that brings the artists, others say the free spirit of seafarers. In Wivenhoe's case it might also be the proximity to the campus of the University of Essex, which was founded in the 1960s and retains its radical academic reputation. The town has a small harbour, a square and a sprinkling of independent shops and cafés. In 1900 it boasted an astonishing twenty pubs; now there are just six, which is still seems like plenty for a small town.

From Wivenhoe we headed inland. We made an utterly futile attempt to take the smallest lanes and ford Alresford Creek to reach Brightlingsea, but ended up riding along the main B-road, which

START: Colchester, Essex • FINISH: Witham, Essex • DISTANCE: 39 miles/63km
TOTAL ASCENT: 149m • TERRAIN: Country lanes and a few stretches of B-road. Easy.

is wide and fairly quiet. From Brightlingsea a small ferry runs across to Mersea Island from April to the end of September. During the winter, when the ferry isn't running, it's best to ride out of Colchester on the other side of the Colne, following the quiet lanes that pass through Fingringhoe.

Somehow the 12 of us – with bikes – managed to cram aboard the ferry for the short crossing to Mersea Island, where we landed on a beach covered in pearl-white oyster shells. This is one of the few good swimming spots on the island, as elsewhere it can be very muddy – particularly at low tide, when the sea retreats into the distance, leaving behind acres of thick ooze (exactly the habitat oysters love).

Like a ramshackle battalion disgorged from a landing craft, we hauled our bikes up the beach and rode along a track to where the road began. Accumulated deposits from the estuary make for fertile farmland, and every scrap of land on the island that didn't have a house built on it was growing crops. We stopped in West Mersea to buy bread and a couple of bottles of wine and rolled downhill to the docks, ready for a shellfish bonanza. The best place to eat is the Company Shed, but it is small and such is its fame that it can get very full, especially on fine weekends. A take-away counter sells unopened

oysters (and a host of other local fish and shellfish) for those who want to beat the queues and enjoy a picnic on the grass, though an oyster knife and a little know-how are recommended.

We ordered several dozen Colchester Natives, the very same species, and from the same waters, as those celebrated by the Romans. Unfortunately, the following summer, it seems the natives experienced a poor spawning season and the public fishery was closed indefinitely in response. Richard Haward, a seventh-generation oyster fisherman whose family mollusc empire includes the Company Shed, assured me that boom and bust is nothing new and he fully expected the stocks to recover before too long. In the meantime, he is still harvesting and selling a small quantity of Natives from his own beds, and there are plenty of rock oysters to be had.

Replete after lunch, we somewhat lethargically got back on the bikes and rode back up through the town and off the island, over The Strood, a 7th-century Saxon causeway that connects Mersea Island to the rest of Essex. The causeway floods at high tide, which can make for an exciting race against the rising waters. Back on the mainland, we continued through several small villages that share the unlucky distinction of having suffered major damage in the

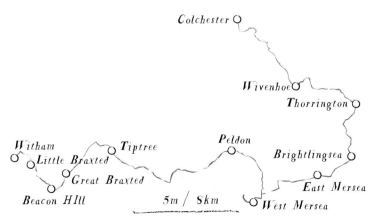

most destructive earthquake to have hit the British Isles in the last four centuries. The 'Great English Earthquake' struck in April 1884, measuring 4.6 on the Richter scale and terrifying the population.

Tiptree, our next stopping point, is a name familiar at breakfast tables across the country. It is as British as the marmalade that is made in huge quantities here by Wilkin & Sons, alongside other jams, jellies and sauces of every kind. Many of them are made from the produce of the 850 acres of fruit farms that surround the village; local production and heritage fruit varieties held sway here long before they became marketing buzzwords. The company runs a museum of preserve-making paraphernalia at the factory, with an adjoining tea room where the most English of high teas are served.

From Tiptree we followed National Cycle Route 16 towards Witham, along quiet lanes lined with hedgerows erupting in clouds of snow-white blackthorn blossom. The cycle route we were following took us through Little Braxted, home to one of the tiniest yet most extraordinary churches in Essex. The building is Norman but the interior was completely redecorated in the late 19th century in the richly ornate Gothic Revival style pioneered by Pugin. It's the work of the local vicar, the Reverend Ernest Geldart, who eventually gave up his religious calling to focus on architecture, designing schemes for several more Essex churches. The interior of the church is a riot of wildly colourful paintings, tiles, wall coverings and inscriptions, almost Islamic in its complex ornamentation.

The visual disorientation that began in the church reached a climax as Cycle Route 16 led us onto a bridge over the A12 and into Witham through an industrial park of giant, windowless hangars, under the railway line and along the edge of the town's allotments. We were fully aware that we'd entered our final destination, once a prosperous centre of the wool trade and briefly a popular spa resort, by the ugly route. But we'd done enough riding for the day and were glad to see the railway station. What's more, I had an extra dozen take-away oysters sneakily tucked away in my pannier, and I was anxious to get them home and into the fridge.

Download route info at thebikeshow.net/24OR

PUBS & PIT STOPS

TUDOR TEA ROOMS 2 High Street, Wivenhoe CO7 9BJ (01206 822824) Quality home-baked cakes and pastries, also breakfasts and lunches.

THE WATERSIDE FISH & CHIPS 59 Waterside, Brightlingsea, Colchester CO7 0AX (01206 302710) Perfectly placed when waiting for the ferry to arrive.

THE COMPANY SHED 129 Coast Road, West Mersea CO5 8PA (01206 382700) Justifiably legendary oyster and seafood shack; bring your own bread and wine. Be prepared to wait, and to pay by cash or cheque – no cards.

TIPTREE TEA ROOMS Brook Road, Tiptree CO5 0RF (01621 814524) Tea rooms attached to the jam factory museum.

THE COMPASSES 12 Colchester Road, Great Totham CM9 8BZ (01621 891238) Slightly off the route, but a good country pub serving hearty food.

BIKE SHOPS: Colchester Cycle Stores, 50 St. Johns St, Colchester CO2 7AD (01206 563890); Cycle King, 46a East Street, Colchester, Essex CO1 2TG (01206 867756); R&A Cycles, The Spinning Wheel, 16 Barfield Road, West Mersea CO5 8QT (01206 384013)

West Mersea

Colchester Native oysters

JOY OF ESSEX

Stunningly picturesque villages, windmills and quiet lanes lined with rare wildflowers -
there's a lot more to north-east Essex than Stansted Airport

———

Essex is the most maligned of counties. Close to London, there's more than a grain of truth in the stereotypes of boy racers and glamour girls; anyone who visits Basildon or Billericay in search of mock mansions, nail bars and glitzy nightclubs will not be disappointed. But Essex is big, and boasts some stunning landscapes and a wealth of architecture and history. Picturesque half-timbered villages, rolling farmland, rivers, windmills, meadows and ancient woodlands: in short, the unmistakable English lowland scene.

This ride began one summer dawn. A friend and I had ridden out of London along the River Lee and wild-camped in a field not far north of Bamber's Green. We woke early to the sound of the first planes coming in to land at Stansted airport, barely a mile away. If the planned expansion of the airport goes ahead, the spot where we camped will be bang in the middle of its second runway. After the planes came the sun, a plump, perfect orb creeping up through the trees into a clear sky. Packing up our gear we were on the road by 7am.

Before long we were riding the narrow lanes towards the upper reaches of the River Chelmer. At Tilty there once stood a large Cistercian abbey, now reduced to a few rubble walls in a field. A small chapel belonging to the monastery survives as the parish church, and the exquisitely carved

tracery in its east window is a tantalising hint of the abbey's lost splendour. The words 'dissolution' and 'reformation' somehow fail to capture the violence with which so many irreplaceable buildings, books and works of art were destroyed through politics and greed.

We continued up the Chelmer to Thaxted, the small town where many of the roads in the area converge. It's a fine place with a windmill on a hill and a stunning half-timbered guildhall. Gustav Holst lived here while composing his *Planets* suite and among his local friends was the Reverend Conrad Noel, the local vicar and a socialist firebrand. As well as hanging the red flag and the flag of Sinn Féin alongside that of St George in his church, the 'Red Vicar' also championed the revival of folk music traditions and, in particular, Morris dancing. It seems all of a piece with the socialist Clarion cycling clubs of the same era, who saw bicycling as the route to freedom, fellowship and a more egalitarian society. Clarion Clubs still exist today, and Thaxted still hosts an annual Morris festival that includes a local version of the remarkable Abbots Bromley Horn Dance, originally from Staffordshire, and performed by six men carrying reindeer horns, with a fool, a hobby horse and a man dressed as Maid Marian. From Thaxted we rolled east and deeper into

---

START & FINISH: Elsenham, Essex • DISTANCE: 38 miles/62km • TOTAL ASCENT: 243m
TERRAIN: Mostly lanes with a few short sections of B-roads. Moderate.

Essex, through the Bardfields, Little and Great, and along the quiet lanes to Finchingfield, a village often called the loveliest in England. Its large, sloping village green, church on a hill, duck pond, windmill and red-tiled Georgian and medieval cottages have been endlessly photographed, but on that day we were the only people around. Sitting in the sun enjoying a late breakfast of coffee and croissants it was all pretty perfect.

We rolled on north, along a long and narrow, gently rising lane. With very few hedgerows, we had fine views across the fields on either side, crops billowing in the breeze. It ranks among the most magical lost lanes I know and I've ridden it often. One February, with dusk approaching, I was mesmerised by a barn owl drifting in long and looping flight over the field beside me and into the setting sun. It is designated a 'protected lane', in

The Fox Inn, Finchingfield

part because of a colony of Essex oxlips. This very rare variety of primula resembles a cross between the much more common cowslip and primrose, and its bright yellow, delicate trumpets can be seen on the verges in the spring.

Sadly, the lane ends at the B1054, a somewhat busier road that took us west through Hempstead (birthplace of the famous highwayman Dick Turpin) as far as Radwinter. From here it was back onto lanes again through Wimbish Green and past a disused RAF airfield that was home to fighter aircraft throughout the second world war. By this point we were heading full steam for the train station at Elsenham.

Just after the railway bridge near Ugley we passed a row of very basic bungalows, built and still owned by a group of East London cycling clubs. Back in the 1930s club members would ride up here from the city for weekends in the countryside, and a local woman let them camp on her land. After the war she gifted them a plot sandwiched between the road and the railway line, where they built their club huts. Despite their ever-dwindling memberships, the clubs still use

them and put on regular *Up the Uts* rides (the 'h' in these huts is always silent), which are open to all and cover much of this lovely, too often over-looked part of Essex.

Download route info at thebikeshow.net/25JE

PUBS & PIT STOPS

POPPY'S TEA ROOM 5 Fishmarket Street, Thaxted CM6 2PG (01371 830453) Award-winning tea shop.

PICTURE POT TEA SHOP The Green, Finchingfield CM7 4JS (01371 811009) Coffee and cake on the prettiest of village greens.

THE FOX INN The Green, Finchingfield CM7 4JX (01371 810151) Upmarket dining, rooms for overnight stays.

THE BLUEBELL INN High Street, Hempstead CB10 2PD (01799 599199) Unpretentious family-run free house serving hearty food; reputedly the exact birthplace of Dick Turpin.

FLEUR DE LYS High Street, Widdington CB11 3SG (01799 543280) Handsome oak-beamed country pub.

No.26

SUN, SEA & SUFFOLK

The elusive beauty of the Suffolk coast lies in its soft, ethereal light,
wide open spaces, distinctive architecture and quiet, unspoiled villages

———

Like many London cyclists, I'd only ever found myself at Dunwich, on the Suffolk coast, in a state of sleep deprivation and physical exhaustion after the annual night ride from London Fields (*see* Ride No. 31). My usual routine is to take a dip in the sea, fall asleep on the beach, eat breakfast and get on the coach home. But this year I decided to stick around and explore another of Britain's vanishing coastlines (*see* also Ride Nos. 4 and 23).

I say vanishing, but the truth is that Dunwich has already vanished. It was once one of the ten largest towns in the country, with 800 houses, a fine deep-water harbour, a guildhall and as many as eight churches. But Dunwich was lost to the seas over a period of several hundred years that began on three fateful January nights in 1286, when storm surges swept away the lowest-lying parts of town and partially blocked the river. The town soldiered on through more surges the following winter, but in 1328 an even more ferocious storm finally blocked the harbour with a huge bank of sand and shingle. Shipping moved up the coast to Walberswick, reducing the tax revenues that Dunwich needed to maintain its sea defences. This was the start of a slow spiral of decline, and by the middle of the 18th century what little remained of the town was finally abandoned to the ever-advancing waves.

The Victorians are remembered as great builders and restorers, but they were also enthralled by the romance of the ruin. J.M.W. Turner painted the lost town's last church, with its imposing tower, standing precariously on the edge of the cliff, and visitors flocked to Dunwich to see it themselves. It finally toppled onto the beach in 1919. Some of the remains were removed to the new church that sits among the few houses, pub and museum that comprise the Dunwich of the 21st century.

We left the shade of our wooded campsite on the cliffs and rode north towards Walberswick through the scented pine plantations that fringe the shoreline. When we reached the road to Blythburgh we turned right towards the coast, taking a shortcut through the woods on a wide, fairly smooth bridleway. It felt good to leave the lanes behind for a while, quiet though they were, and immerse ourselves in the sounds of the woods. We emerged onto a more open heath, punctuated by thickets: probably an old hunting ground of Westwood Lodge, a rambling red brick Elizabethan manor house whose elaborate chimneys rise up above its gabled roofs.

Walberswick, once a thriving port and fierce rival to Dunwich, now has a sleepy, artsy feel, with tar-blackened timber shacks on the beach and a gently sloping village green lined with red brick

---

START & FINISH: Dunwich, Suffolk • DISTANCE: 44 miles/71km • TOTAL ASCENT: 180m
TERRAIN: Country lanes with short off-road sections that can be muddy after heavy rain. Moderate.

Walberswick

cottages, tea shops and a general store. It looked like a perfect place to spend a day lounging on the beach, with a spot of crabbing from the bridge, kite-flying or a dip in the sea thrown in. Anyone looking for more excitement could hop on the rowing-boat ferry across the river to fashionable, upmarket Southwold.

We rode inland along a narrow, raised track by the side of the river, past bright boats moored at countless jetties, before turning onto the road across the marshes and then taking a series of lanes and paths through the woods to Blythburgh. In this village on the very edge of firm land stands the Holy Trinity Church, affectionately known as the Cathedral of the Marshes. It was built in the 15th century, on the site of earlier churches going as far back as the 7th century, when the site was used for the burial of East Anglian royalty. Beyond its dramatic location and sheer scale, the most notable feature of the church is the timbered roof with beautifully carved angels in flight, looking down on the mortals below. Somehow, the angels escaped the Puritan iconoclasts who destroyed so much fine art during the Reformation (and who would be horrified to find the church is now used for classical concerts as well as worship). The years have faded the angels; originally they would have been brightly painted in red and green and spangled with silver and gold foil.

From Blythburgh we continued inland between cornfields, as the midday heat burned off the sea haze and revealed the gently rolling landscape in bright summer sunshine. Just a few lonely white clouds drifted in from the west, deepening the sapphire sky. The landscape is pleasant rather than spectacular, but it's easy riding and we stopped to explore the villages on the way. Bramfield church is unusual for its thatched roof and round tower, which is detached from and older than the church. Inside, a series of carved heads, including a pig and a green man, adorn the

arches. 'Silly Suffolk' is alive and well in Peasenhall, which hosts an annual Pea Festival every July, featuring the World Pea Podding Championships, pea shooting, pea throwing and 'ten pea bowling'.

From Bruisyard, which has another of Suffolk's distinctive round church towers, we followed the route of the River Alde all the way to the mouth of its estuary at Snape. The large, rambling buildings on the quay were built as malthouses, for converting barley to brewer's malt by soaking, sprouting and drying it. Since 1969 they have been the headquarters of Aldeburgh's festival of classical music, founded after the second world war by the composer Benjamin Britten. Britten had first bought a home in the area here in Snape in the 1930s, where he composed his opera *Peter Grimes* – fittingly, since the story comes from a work by Aldeburgh-born poet George Crabbe.

As the afternoon faded into evening, we turned north, passing the ruins of Leiston Abbey, another memorial to the political upheavals of the Reformation. After the dissolution, most

of the abbey fell to ruins, but a farm and later Georgian additions were built onto it. The ruins are an English Heritage site and free to visit, but the building is now home to a chamber-music academy; as we walked among the ruins the sound of a string ensemble drifted across fields darkened by lengthening shadows, swallows high overhead.

With a few miles still to go, we pushed on across the Minsmere marshes as darkness crept up around us, and rode along a rough track through the dense, dark woods that lead up to Westleton Heath. We'd been hot all day under the sun, but suddenly the air was chilly and dew was falling on the fields. Stepping up the pace, we pulled on every piece of clothing we had and raced the last downhill mile back to Dunwich and supper at the pub. By the time we returned to our campsite, the sky was a deep, dark blue, with only the inky silhouettes of the trees above our tent showing darker, and the moon casting its silvery light over the heath.

Download route info at thebikeshow.net/26SS

PUBS & PIT STOPS

PARISH LANTERN TEA ROOMS The Green, Walberswick IP18 6TT (01502 723173) Friendly tea room serving lunches in a pretty walled garden.

THE STAR INN Hall Road, Wenhaston IP19 9HF (01502 478240). Old-fashioned interiors, home cooking and a sunny garden.

THE SIBTON WHITE HORSE INN Halesworth Road, Sibton IP17 2JJ (01728 660337) Village pub known for its gourmet food, with rooms for overnight stays.

THE WEAVERS TEA ROOM 2 The Knoll, Peasenhall IP17 2JE (01728 660548) Cakes and cream teas at a classic English tea-room with an outdoor terrace.

EMMETT'S STORE The Street, Peasenhall IP17 2HJ (01728 660250). Award-winning cafe and delicatessen, smoking Suffolk ham since 1820. A foodie paradise.

ALDE GARDEN The White Horse Inn, Low Road, Sweffling IP17 2BB (01728 664178). Small is beautiful at this lovely family-run campsite with yurts, gypsy caravans and a tiny pub.

THE SHIP Dunwich IP17 3DT (01728 648219) Good cheer at an inn serving good, locally-sourced food, with well-appointed rooms for overnight stays.

CLIFF HOUSE HOLIDAY PARK Minsmere Road, Dunwich IP17 3DQ (01728 648282) Large cliff-top campsite that manages to feel secluded. Good restaurant, cycle hire.

BIKE SHOP: Byways Bicycles, Priory Farm, Darsham IP17 3QD (01728 668764)

BIKE HIRE: Cliff House Holiday Park (see listing above); Byways Bicycles (see bike shop listing above); Eastbridge Cycle Hire Company, The Eel's Foot Inn, Eastbridge IP16 4SN (01728 830154)

Dunwich Heath

Holy Trinity, Blythburgh

No.27

WAVENEY WEEKENDER

The soft, clear waters of the Waveney are perfect for a quick dip on a ride along the Norfolk–Suffolk border that follows in the tyre tracks of nature writer and wild swimmer Roger Deakin

———

The late environmentalist Roger Deakin loved the River Waveney, and – as anyone who's read *Waterlog*, his acclaimed account of a swim across Britain, will know – Deakin knew his rivers. He lived not far from Diss and treasured the sweet waters of his local river, which flows for 60 miles across East Anglia, separating Norfolk from Suffolk. When not wild swimming or tramping through woodlands, Deakin rode his bike along the lanes around his home, and he considered all of these 'subversive activities' that 'allow us to regain a sense of what is old and wild in these islands, by getting off the beaten track and breaking free of the official version of things.' I couldn't put it better.

We were going to a midsummer birthday party in Bungay, a market town on the Waveney and decided that instead of taking the train, we'd make a long weekend of it by riding up. The last section of our ride from Diss to Bungay was by far the most scenic and makes for an excellent weekend round-trip, as the fast train between London and Norwich stops at Diss.

On the way out of Diss we took a short cut along a track past a large field lined with corrugated tin huts and pink clusters of tiny, playful piglets trotting and tumbling, while their gigantic mothers rooted about in the earth or rested motionless on their sides. Pigs are big business in this part of East Anglia, and it was good to see these animals enjoying the freedom of an outdoor life.

We passed the edge of Hoxne, a pretty village whose wide main street and large church give a clue to days gone by when the place was altogether more busy and bustling. Back in the middle of the 19th century, Hoxne had almost 1,500 inhabitants and supported three pubs, two beerhouses, a grocer, a chemist, a draper, four shoemakers, three blacksmiths, a tailor, two saddlers, a wheelwright, a butcher, a miller, a surgeon and three schools. The population has halved since then, and it's a microcosm of how people and economic life in Britain as a whole have left the villages and moved to cities and towns.

Leaving the B-road just past Hoxne and turning onto a narrow, shady lane, we felt the river before we saw it. There was a damp chill in the air as we rounded the lush, steep slopes where the river cuts its way around Syleham House. We crossed over the river into Norfolk and followed a quiet, flat lane along the Waveney's flood plain. This was once the main road along the valley, but most traffic now uses the new, faster A143 which runs parallel, so we could happily ride along two abreast.

START & FINISH: Diss, Norfolk • DISTANCE: 48 miles/77km • TOTAL ASCENT: 183m
TERRAIN: Country lanes and a short section of B-road. Moderate.

In an account of a journey down the river in a canoe, Deakin wrote 'with its secret pools and occasional sandy beaches, the Waveney is full of swimming holes, diving stages improvised from wooden pallets, dangling ropes, and upturned canoes pulled up on the bank. Every two or three miles you come to a weir and a white-washed watermill.' The river runs high between flower-studded banks, and it's easy to just slip in and sample its deep, soft, sweet waters. The simplest and best plan is to follow a path from the road down to the water's edge and jump in; it may require scouting out a riverside footpath or bridleway or hopping over a fence or through a gate. Even if it might in some places be strictly trespass, it's very unlikely anyone will mind. I enjoyed swimming upstream past green-and-yellow reefs of water buttercup, then lying on my back and drifting back downstream.

River Waveney, near Mendham

Bungay is a good-looking Suffolk town with a triangular market place, the remains of a large early medieval castle, and an imposing church with dressed flint walls. In 1577 the church is said to have seen the most dramatic appearance of the infamous Black Dog or Black Shuck, which has inspired the name of the local marathon and the local football team, the town coat of arms and a song by glam-rock band The Darkness. In 1688 a fire destroyed most of the town, but the people of Bungay rebuilt and prospered in the Georgian era. The town attracted wealthy, fashionable visitors and was even dubbed 'Little London' on account of its sophisticated entertainments and elegant buildings. Today it has plenty of independent shops and a row of antique specialist. The overall air is of confidence and quiet contentment and it still makes for a good place for an overnight stay.

For the return journey to Diss we rode south towards a cluster of small villages and hamlets named after their churches and collectively known as The Saints. Among them, we stopped in at St

Peter's Hall, an exquisite moated manor house that's now home to a microbrewery and a bar with an exceptionally grand dining room in the the main hall. The lanes were almost empty and took us on a gently rolling journey through arable fields, with occasional views down into the valley.

Back down on the river at Syleham we retraced our course upstream until Hoxne, where we made a turn to head south. On the way out of Hoxne on the road to Cross Street is Goldbrook Bridge. To look at, it's not especially interesting, but legend has it that this is where Edmund, the 9th-century king of East Anglia, was captured and killed by invading Vikings. In the years that followed, a powerful cult grew up around the memory of Edmund as an early Anglo-Saxon king-martyr, and his burial shrine at the abbey of Bury St Edmunds attracted countless pilgrims. St Edmund was the patron saint of England for two centuries until St George (a Greek soldier in the Roman army who never set foot in Britain), was given the role during the Crusades. More recently, the self-appointed Knights of St Edmund invoked the medieval curse of the saint against the property developers and retailers behind the new shopping centre in Bury St Edmunds.

From Hoxne we could have ridden back to Diss the way we came, but we had enough time to take a longer, alternative route via Eye and Mellis. This last village was home to Roger Deakin until he died, and much of the area is described with his beautiful, light touch in the collected *Notes from Walnut Tree Farm*. Deakin combined writing and broadcasting with ecological activism. Showing that campaigning can make a difference both globally and locally, he worked on Greenpeace's powerful anti-whaling campaigns and at the same time successfully mobilised his neighbours to save and protect Cowpasture Lane, a historic drover's track, now a green lane, that was threatened with obliteration by a local farmer. Deakin also helped to found Common Ground, a charity devoted to linking nature with culture through the celebration of local distinctiveness.

Deakin's many bicycle rides in and around his area were mostly short and undertaken simply for the fun of it. It's clear he loved the way that his bike brought him closer to nature and the changing seasons, as well as offering a more sociable way to travel. It's also quite clear that regular bike rides played an important part in Deakin's creative process. In one diary entry he writes that 'the artist doesn't just sit in the studio waiting for the painting to come to him – and nor do I when I write this piece – I shake it out of myself on a bike ride.' Anyone who has ever experienced a lightbulb moment while out riding a bike will know exactly what he means.

Download route info at thebikeshow.net/27WW

PUBS & PIT STOPS

THE SWAN INN Hoxne IP21 5AS (01379 668275) 15th century, timbered pub with large garden.

THE BLACK SWAN Church Lane, Homersfield IP20 0ET (01986 788204) Old coaching inn with simple campsite in a field by the river.

EARSHAM STREET CAFÉ 11–13 Earsham Street, Bungay, NR35 1AE (01986 893103). Coffee, cake and light lunches with a garden out back.

CASTLE INN 35 Earsham Street, Bungay NR35 1AF (01986 892283). Stylish inn with four rooms and mouth-watering food.

ST. PETER'S HALL St. Peter South Elmham NR35 1NQ (01986 782322) Microbrewery with restaurant and bar in a moated manor house.

FOXHOLE B&B Fox Cottage, Fox Hill, St Cross South Elmham IP20 0NX (01986 888180) Tiny ex-village-pub offering just one (en-suite) room for B&B.

EYE FISH AND CHIP SHOP 6 Lambseth Street, Eye IP23 7AG (01379 870378) Old-school chippy.

BIKE SHOPS: Madgetts Cycle, 8 Shelfanger Road, Diss IP22 4EH (01379 650419); MG Cycles, 2B Earsham St, Bungay NR35 1AG (01986 892985)

BIKE HIRE: The Cycle Shack, 1 Chapel St, Diss IP22 4AN (01379 641212)

LONDON

AN EASTERN EXCURSION

Twenty almost traffic-free miles around the rapidly changing, intensely urban east London, with some breathtaking views along the way

———

I first devised this route for a 'Philosophy by Bicycle' ride organised by the School of Life, a London enterprise that holds courses, talks and events based around 'good ideas for everyday life'. My good idea was a largely traffic-free route for about twenty people around some spectacular but unfamiliar parts of London. Along the way, the philosophy writer and broadcaster Nigel Warburton would lead discussions about the nature of self, space, free will, fear and death – the last, appropriately enough, after walking our bikes under the Thames in a narrow Victorian foot tunnel. This east London excursion is a firm favourite of mine, especially when visitors come to town. After they've had their fill of the usual tourist sights, they're always wowed by this alternative take on the world's greatest city.

Broadway Market typifies the transformation of the London borough of Hackney from a dismissed, run-down area to the centre of a buzzing, creative quarter of London. There is still a lot of deprivation in the borough, and those who argue that 'gentrification' doesn't actually benefit local people do have a point. Whatever the pros and cons, the changes are there to see and never more clearly than on a Saturday morning, when Broadway Market is rammed with vendors of organic vegetables, artisan breads, single-estate olive oils and the other accoutrements of enlightened urban living in the early 21st century, flanked by fashionable shops and cafés on either side.

Bicycling figure prominently in Hackney's transformation, and Hackney Cyclists have been effective in convincing the authorities to prioritise cycling and walking over motorised travel. Anyone standing on the Cat and Mutton bridge over the Regent's Canal at the south end of Broadway Market could be forgiven for thinking they were in bike-loving Amsterdam, not bike-cautious London.

I met two friends for a coffee at Lock 7, the café and bike shop next to the bridge and we set out eastwards under a clear autumn sky along the Regent's Canal. Deep blue skies above trees turning golden-yellow and rich auburn must be nature's way of dispelling the gloom that accompanies the end of summer. It's a visual treat and worked wonders on our moods as we rode along chatting, wrapped up warm in scarves and gloves.

It's possible to ride into Victoria Park and follow National Cycle Route 1, but we chose to stay on the towpath, making a left turn just past Old Ford Lock and joining the Hertford Canal, which in turn connects to the River Lee Navigation. The transformation of Broadway Market is nothing compared with what's happened on the far side of the river with the construction of the 2012 Olympic Park. We had a good view of the stadium as we rode onto

---

START & FINISH: Broadway Market, Hackney • DISTANCE: 21 miles/33km • TOTAL ASCENT: 37m
TERRAIN: Canal towpath, surfaced cycle tracks and a few quieter urban roads. Easy.

Royal Albert Dock

Lee Navigation

the elevated path of the Greenway, a walking and cycling route that offers wide, sweeping vistas over east London.

The Greenway runs along the top of a huge embankment, under which lies a giant sewage pipe, part of the network devised by Victorian engineer Joseph Bazalgette to address the 'great stinks' of the 1850s. One of his descendants is Peter Bazalgette, creator of the *Big Brother* television show, and local wags quip that while Joseph devoted himself to taking the effluent out of people's homes, Peter has made a fortune by putting it back in. The large, ornate, neo-Byzantine building on the right of the Greenway is not an Eastern Orthodox church but the old Abbey Mills pumping station. The Victorians held strongly to the belief that cleanliness is next to godliness, and this might offer some explanation of this extraordinary building, which was nicknamed the Cathedral of Sewage. The interior appears as the terrifying Arkham Asylum in the film *Batman Begins*.

Shortly after passing the modern blocks of Newham Hospital we left the Greenway and turned south, crossing the busy A13 by bridge and riding through Beckton District Park, an unexpectedly wild green corridor that took us all the way to the Royal Albert Dock. Rolling up to the water's edge and looking across to London City Airport and the skyline around to Canary Wharf is one of London's 'big-sky moments' and never fails to impress. Out on the water a dragon boat team was training and, right on cue, an aircraft appeared out of nowhere to touch down with a puff of tyre rubber and the roar of engines in reverse.

The Royal Albert Dock was opened in 1880 as one of three connected mega-docks that specialised in the unloading of meat, tobacco and fruit and vegetables, as well as berthing the biggest passenger liners of the times. Traffic through the docks reached its peak in the boom years after the second world war, but after that their demise was rapid as ever-larger ships, containerisation and direct-to-rail technologies favoured competing docks downstream at Tilbury. The docks

closed in 1981 and have been slowly adapting to new uses, a process that continues to this day.

Some day it may be possible to cycle the length of the quayside, but we had to pick our way past the gleaming new offices of Newham Council and duck through the Cyprus station of the Docklands Light Railway to emerge once again at the water's edge among the curious cylindrical buildings of the University of East London. After riding over the bridge at the mouth of the dock we were soon at North Woolwich and racing along the riverside path to catch the free ferry that was just arriving at the quay. The ferry pirouettes on the tide across the Thames in a short crossing that never fails to feel satisfyingly nautical. Londoners have workaholic sewerage maestro Joseph Bazalgette to thank again; as head of the Metropolitan Board of Works, he gave the green light to the free ferry idea back in 1884.

Once on the south side of the Thames we were heading back into the city, past the titanium-coated shells of the Thames Barrier, which bring a futuristic glimmer to the industrial grime of this wide reach of the river. When the wind is right, the smell of burnt caramel drifts across from the Tate and Lyle sugar refinery. We stopped for a gargantuan roast lunch at the Anchor and Hope, sitting outside in the warm sunshine, an unusual pleasure in early November.

From here, National Cycle Route 4 hugs the river as far as the continual construction sites allow.

The Dome seems to have recovered from its humiliating millennial debut and found its niche as a concert venue. It sits at the tip of the North Greenwich peninsula, a slightly tacky development in an island of car parks, motorways and abandoned concrete, and is best reached by the Thames Clipper service, a fast ferry that sails downstream from central London. Our appetite for gritty urban landscapes was beginning to flag, so we were glad to arrive at the Georgian splendours of Greenwich, which was (as ever) heaving with tourists. There's a lot to see and do in Greenwich, but time was marching on so we headed back over the Thames – or rather under it, through the foot tunnel, pushing our bikes as cycling's not allowed down there.

On the north side of the river we crossed the Isle of Dogs, an island formed by one of the Thames's largest meanders around its south side and the docks on its northern edge. It's a mixture of flash City wealth and some of London's poorest housing estates, with a city farm, Mudchute, in the midde of it all. The towers of Canary Wharf are so often seen from afar that it feels uncanny riding right up to them, but National Cycle Route 1 does just that before negotiating the busy Westferry Circus and entering the calm of Mile End Park. There was little to see so late in the year, but the wildflower meadows at the park's south end are the best in London. The park, built in the late 1990s on a swathe of the city that was bombed during the war, is an ecological treasure trove of meadows, wetlands and a tree-lined 'green bridge' over the Mile End Road.

Cities never stand still, but the east of London has changed more than most in recent decades. Our ride was not on lost lanes of countryside variety, but rather on a cycling-friendly green chain. Free from the tyranny of motor traffic, this chain is reviving nature and restoring tranquillity in the most heavily populated and intensively used parts of London, showing how the city can be made a more pleasant place to live and work. A route designed for a day of philosophy by bicycle could easily double up as a rolling seminar in urban design and regeneration.

Download route info at thebikeshow.net/28EE

PUBS & PIT STOPS

LOCK 7 CYCLE CAFÉ 129 Pritchards Road E2 9AP (020 7739 3042) Friendly workshop and shop with a café alongside the bikes.

PAVILION CAFÉ Victoria Park E9 7DE (020 8980 0030) Excellent food at this café by the lake.

VIEW TUBE The Greenway E15 2PJ (020 3130 0469) A stack of bright green shipping containers with a lovely little café and a great view of the Olympic Park.

ANCHOR AND HOPE Riverside SE7 7SS (020 8858 0382) Friendly, unpretentious riverside boozer serving trad pub food in huge quantities.

CUTTY SARK Ballast Quay, Greenwich SE10 9PD (020 8858 3146) Georgian pub in a perfect riverside location.

PALM TREE Mile End Park E3 5BH (020 8980 2918) Atmospheric canalside pub improbably surrounded by acres of wildflower meadow.

BIKE SHOPS: Lock 7 (see listing above); Harry Perry Cycles, 88 Powis Street, Woolwich SE18 6LQ (020 8854 2383); Evans Cycles, Canary Wharf E14 5EZ (020 7516 0094)

BIKE HIRE: Greenwich Cycle Rental, 95 Old Woolwich Road SE10 9PP (0789 1374638; office hours 020 8858 6677)

Woolwich Ferry

Greenwich Foot Tunnel

No.29

GARDEN CITY

Joining the dots between central London's amazing
diversity of gardens, parks and green spaces

———

With more than 3,000 parks and open spaces covering 67 square miles, London has a fair claim to be the world's greenest big city. Even if rampant property prices put a garden out of reach, summer lunchtimes see London office workers spill out into the city's many parks, kick off their shoes and enjoy a precious half hour in the sun.

London's really big parks were originally royal hunting grounds and then places for private entertainment. The democratisation of the city's parks took off in the 18th century, and Lambeth was at the heart of it, from the pleasure gardens at Vauxhall to Cuper's tea gardens and Curtis' botanical gardens in Waterloo. It makes sense that the world's first museum of garden history should be in Lambeth, in a disused church that is also the final resting place of the John Tradescants, father and son, legendary plant-hunters who introduced so many of the exotic species that fill those gardens. It is right next door to Lambeth Palace, home and garden of the Archbishop of Canterbury, and that's where we met to begin a ride around central London's green spaces.

Setting off across Lambeth Bridge we took in the classic 'News at Ten' view across to the Houses of Parliament, and after crossing Millbank we followed the back streets through Smith Square towards Westminster Abbey. In Dean's Yard is the entrance to the College Garden (free and open all year, but only certain weekdays). It is said to be Britain's oldest garden in continuous cultivation, dating back 900 years and originally used by the monastery to grow medicinal herbs; the Abbey was founded even earlier, in the 7th century, when the land here was a brambly, overgrown island in the Thames.

The present Abbey is an imposing Gothic battleship whose construction began in 1245 and took nearly 300 years to complete, with the two western towers added by Nicholas Hawksmoor in the 18th century. Ever since King Harold was crowned there, and soon after William the Conqueror, it's been the favourite place for coronations, royal weddings and burials. Lying alongside a host of kings and queens are luminaries of civic life and, most famously, the writers, playwrights and poets buried and commemorated at Poets' Corner in the south transept, as well as the Tomb of the Unknown Soldier.

After crossing busy Victoria Street, we set out across a sequence of Royal Parks that offer a traffic-free route from Westminster all the way to Notting Hill. St James's Park is the oldest and lies on former marshland drained by Henry VIII to provide a park for hunting deer. James I turned the park into a menagerie with camels, crocodiles,

---

START: Garden Museum, Lambeth • FINISH: Phoenix Garden, Soho • DISTANCE: 14 miles/22km
TOTAL ASCENT: 119m • TERRAIN: Parks and a few quiet central London roads. Easy.

an elephant and exotic birds. After the Restoration, Charles II remodelled it in the elaborate, formal style he had seen while in exile in France. The park was opened to the public and earned a reputation for wild and depraved sexual antics that inspired the libertine poet the Earl of Rochester to write *A Ramble in St. James's Park*, a poem so extravagantly rude that no English publisher would print it for almost 300 years. The park has since been landscaped in a naturalistic style, and James I's menagerie has transmuted into a thriving population of water fowl on the lake, including a colony of pelicans descended from birds that were a gift of the Russian ambassador in 1664.

On Sunday the Mall is closed to motor traffic and this wide avenue, surfaced in regal red tarmac, is a haven for cyclists, walkers and skaters. Passing the crowds of tourists at Buckingham Palace we rode up Constitution Hill, along the edge of Green Park. Once a haunt of highwaymen and duellists, today the park is a big sloping lawn with a canopy of huge plane trees. London has always been a city of immigrants, not just people but plants as well. None has been as successful as the London plane tree (*Platanus × hispanica*). Originally from Spain, it is extremely hardy and resistant to smog, drought and heavy pruning. Nor does it seem to mind being encased in tarmac.

The busy roundabout at Hyde Park Corner saw some of London's earliest traffic jams as far back as the 1870s, and at rush hour it's just as busy with cyclists streaming across the central island. As one of the city's largest open spaces, Hyde Park has traditionally been the location for London's biggest massed gatherings. Most have been politically inspired crowds, from the Chartists to the Jarrow Marchers and the Stop the War Coalition, but some are more festive, from the Great Exhibition in 1851 to a 1969 concert by the Rolling Stones attended by between 250,000 and 500,000 people.

We rode west through the park along the Rotten Row cycle path, past the gentle, flowing memorial to Diana, Princess of Wales and into Kensington

The Phoenix Garden

Gardens, towards the palace where she lived. We carried on out of the park and up Kensington Palace Gardens, a long, broad avenue lined with grand embassies and ambassadorial residences. After enduring a short stretch of the Bayswater Road (walking the pavement is a reasonable alternative), we were at north end of the Broad Walk and looped back to find our way back to Speakers' Corner at the north-east of Hyde Park. This is where crowds come to debate anything and everything. Centuries ago, much bigger and more bloodthirsty crowds gathered here at the infamous Tyburn Tree, which was not a tree at all but an elaborate gallows for grisly public executions, which allowed up to two dozen people to be hanged simultaneously.

Leaving Hyde Park behind us, we followed an unremarkable backstreet route through Marylebone to St John's Wood, where we joined up with the Regent's Canal, heading east. London's canals serve the city as linear parks and are tranquil places to ride and walk. The towpaths are narrow, so it's important to ride slowly and deploy extreme courtesy at all times, lest bicycles are one day banned – as they already are on some of the stretches of canal around Little Venice. The canal lies in a deep cutting lined by high brick banks, and the trees above were a visual feast of autumn colour. We soon found our way to Regent's Park and, while racing cyclists were doing laps around the Outer Circle, we crossed into the park. We rode past London Zoo, whose 17,000 or so inmates makes it Britain's biggest, and on into through the park along the Broad Walk.

South of the park we turned towards the quiet and elegant Georgian streets of Fitzrovia, cycling past the foot of the BT tower. Built in the 1960s, the slim cylindrical tower was the first building to overtake Sir Christopher Wren's masterpiece, St Paul's Cathedral, as the tallest in London. It now ranks ninth. Fitzrovia and Bloomsbury are two of the areas developed during the 'golden age' of real estate speculation in the 18th century, driven by aristocratic landowners who leased plots of farmland to build great estates for the expanding ranks of well-to-do Londoners. In class-conscious Georgian London, these were originally something like today's gated communities, and though they've all since been opened up to passers by, a handful of the central gardens remain for the exclusive enjoyment of residents.

Riding the segregated cycle route along Torrington Place, we stopped at Gordon Square Garden and Tavistock Gardens, both originally part of the Duke of Bedford's London estate. In the early 20th century these squares were home to the Bloomsbury Set, a wealthy and bohemian group of writers, artists and intellectuals including Virginia Woolf, John Maynard Keynes and E.M. Forster. We then skirted the edge of Coram's Fields, a 7-acre park on the former site of the Foundling Hospital for abandoned children. The site was threatened with development when the hospital moved to the countryside in the 1920s, but a campaign by the local community won the day, and it's been a children's park ever since.

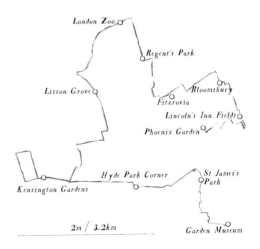

London Zoo

Regent's Park

Lisson Grove

Bloomsbury

Fitzrovia

Lincoln's Inn Fields

Phoenix Garden

Hyde Park Corner

St James's Park

Kensington Gardens

2m / 3.2km

Garden Museum

The Foundling Museum on Brunswick Square remains; as well as an impressive art collection, it still holds the 'foundling tokens' (a button, a swatch of material, even a poem) that were given by mothers leaving their babies so that the hospital could match a mother with her child, should she ever come back to claim it. Most children never saw their mothers again, and their tokens make for a poignant collection of objects.

Car-free Lamb's Conduit Street took us south towards Lincoln's Inn Fields, London's largest public square. On the north side is Sir John Soane's Museum, an exquisite private collection that combines art, architecture, furniture and design. It's free, and an essential visit. After a quick pint at the Seven Stars we turned westwards in the direction of the cobblestone streets of Seven Dials, once a dirty, grotty corner of the city but now a busy commercial neighbourhood of small, independent shops.

Our afternoon roll around central London came to an end at the Phoenix Garden, one of London's smallest but most lovely green spaces. It is tucked among the tall buildings behind Shaftesbury Avenue, on the site of car park that was built on top of a second world war bomb site. Set up in 1984 as a community wildlife garden, its naturalistic planting and colourful floral displays bring an arresting sense of wildness to a small plot of otherwise unremarkable land. It shows more clearly than any of the larger parks we'd visited how plants can transform urban spaces for the better. London is a noisy and crowded city of eight million people and needs its green spaces, every last one of them.

Download route info at thebikeshow.net/29GC

PUBS & PIT STOPS

GARDEN MUSEUM CAFÉ 5 Lambeth Palace Road SE1 7LB (020 7401 8865) Small, informal café serving freshly cooked lunches and cakes.

ROYAL CHINA 13 Queensway, Bayswater W2 4QJ (020 7221 2535) Outstanding dim sum in a cavernous gold-and-black lacquered interior.

MAROUSH EXPRESS 68 Edgware Road W2 2EG (020 7224 9339) Efficient and good value café on London's Lebanese mile.

PATISSERIE DEUX AMIS Judd Street, WC1H 9QT (020 7383 7029) Tiny French café makes for a perfect afternoon tea stop.

SEVEN STARS 53–54 Carey Street WC2A 2JB (020 7242 8521) Small, beguiling 400-year-old pub serving home-cooked food and good beer.

THE ANGEL 61–62 Saint Giles High Street WC2H 8LE (020 7240 2876) Brilliant London boozer with cosy rooms and a fabulous tiled coaching alley.

BIKE SHOPS: Action Bikes, 19 Dacre Street SW1H 0DJ (020 7799 2233); Fitzrovia Bicycles, 136–138 New Cavendish Street W1W 6YD (020 7631 5060); Bikefix, 48 Lamb's Conduit Street WC1N 3LH (020 7405 1218); Evans Cycles, 178 High Holborn, WC1V 7AA (020 7836 5585)

BIKE HIRE: London Bicycle Tour Company, 1 Gabriel's Wharf, 56 Upper Ground, SE1 9PP (020 3318 3088); Barclays Cycle Hire, Lambeth Road and Moor St.

Regent's Canal

Kensington Gardens

WIMBLEDON TO WEYBRIDGE

Parks and the Thames Path make for a scenic, mostly traffic-free escape route from south-west London into Surrey.

———

Vast swathes of south-west London are effectively off-limits to all but the fastest, most courageous cyclists, who are willing to barrel along fast dual carriageways. This is a real shame, since the 'Portsmouth Road' (now the A3 dual carriageway) was a popular thoroughfare for early generations of London cyclists seeking to escape the city for a day in the countryside (*see* Ride No. 12). Fortunately a 'green chain' of large parks, together with the Thames Path, combine into an easy-riding and mostly traffic-free alternative.

We – four grown ups and a toddler, who was sitting securely in a seat mounted onto the front of his mum's bike – began our ride at Wimbledon station, on a bright June morning. Almost immediately we faced a short, sharp hill to reach Wimbledon Common, but I assured everyone that this was the biggest hill of the day, and we were soon back on the flat, freewheeling across the Common. The track runs through a patch of woodland alongside Beverley Brook, a small river that owes its name to the beavers for whom it was once home.

Sadly, these cute and industrious creatures were hunted to extinction nearly 500 years ago. They are being re-introduced in a few rural wetlands and rivers but not, it seems, here in south-west London. For much of the 20th century Beverley Brook flowed with sewage, but there's been something of a clean-up operation going on, and wildlife is now flourishing. Maybe there's hope for the return of the beavers yet, but for now they remain every bit as mythical as the Wombles for which Wimbledon Common is better known.

Crossing the A3 we rode into Richmond Park, the largest of London's royal parks and probably the city's most popular place for cycling. It's a great place to take novice cyclists, and anyone without a bike can hire one by the café at Roehampton Gate. There's a gentle, off-road cycle path that meanders through the trees around the very edge of the park, while the 7-mile road circuit around the perimeter is also ideal for road cyclists. Weekend mornings see large groups of amateur club riders doing laps; top professional David Millar holds the unofficial record of 13 minutes 35 seconds. National Cycle Route 4, which starts in Greenwich, also crosses the park on its way west. We headed into the middle of the park to join the route, and stopped for an ice-cream at a kiosk under the trees.

Richmond Park is beautifully landscaped, and there are parts that feel genuinely wild. It is also home to around 600 red and fallow deer, so the park's trees have characteristic 'browse lines' where deer have nibbled all the leaves and twigs

---

START: Wimbledon, London • FINISH: Weybridge, Surrey • DISTANCE: 19 miles/31km
TOTAL ASCENT: 104m • Terrain: Well-surfaced off-road paths, some quiet suburban roads. Easy.

Hampton Court Palace

they can reach. Deer also eat tree saplings, helping to maintain the wide-open vistas for which the park is best known. During the autumn rutting season, males compete with each other for the right to breed with the females. The clashes, involving loud barking and roaring, and clashes of antlers, are full-on and make for quite a spectacle, though it's unwise to get too close.

At the top of the hill heading west out of the park is an old wooden 'danger board' sign put up by the Cyclists' Touring Club before road signage became a government responsibility. In white letters on a blue background it urges 'Caution' on the steep gradient. At the bottom of the hill lies Ham, an archetypal English village that was enveloped by London's suburban expansion when the new railways offered comfortable and rapid transport from outlying areas into the heart of the metropolis. Nearby Ham House is a large, riverside stately home that's a treasure trove of 17th-century decorative art with fine gardens, restored and maintained by the National Trust (£).

National Cycle Route 4 is mostly well marked and, since it runs alongside the Thames all the way to Weybridge, it's dead easy to follow even where signs are missing. The only confusion arises when getting through Kingston town centre onto Kingston Bridge; if all else fails here, walk. Beyond Kingston there are plenty of places to stop and enjoy the ever-changing scenes of the river life. Rounding the bend in the Thames at Hampton Court is always a thrill. It would be easy to spend a whole day looking around the huge royal palace and its beautifully manicured gardens, making the most of the admission charge. But there's a fair bit to be seen even without paying, including a walled rose garden that's a real feast for the senses.

Having crossed Hampton Court Bridge from the Middlesex to the Surrey bank of the Thames, there's a strong sporting theme all the way along the next stretch, whether on or off the water. The river runs right past East Molesey cricket ground, where really big hitters can try to send the ball over the trees into the drink. A little further

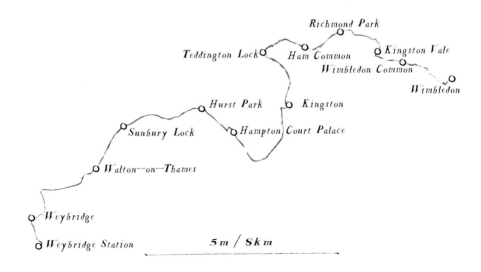

upstream is Moulsey Hurst (now Hurst Park), one of England's oldest sporting venues, from possibly England's first game of golf to prize-fighting, horse-racing and archery. It's notable among cricket buffs as the first place where a batsman was dismissed 'leg before wicket', back in 1795.

The cycle route along the Thames continues on up the river to Runnymede, where it heads inland across Windsor Great Park (*see* Ride No. 10) and from there on to Reading, Bristol and all the way to the western tip of Wales. But on this day, Weybridge made a sensible journey's end for us. We had taken it easy but covered nearly 20 miles, almost all of it in traffic-free tranquillity, and in doing so we'd seen a different side of south-west London from the busy trunk roads and suburban sprawl. Our toddler had shown just how relaxed he was on the bike by falling fast asleep.

Download route info at thebikeshow.net/30WW

PUBS & PIT STOPS

THE BOATER'S INN Lower Ham Rd, Kingston-upon-Thames, KT2 5AU (020 8541 4672) Riverside pub popular with Kingston Wheelers, the local cycling club.

KINGSTON offers plenty of choice, including shops for picnic supplies.

COFFEE BAY East Molesey Cricket Club KT8 9AL Simple outdoor café, overlooking the river and the cricket ground.

THE SWAN 50 Manor Rd, Walton-on-Thames KT12 2PF (01932 225964) A popular riverside pub.

BIKE SHOPS: Smith Bros, 14A Church Road, Wimbledon Village SW19 5DL (020 8946 2270); Sigma Sport, 37–43 High Street, Hampton Wick KT1 4DA (020 8614 9777); East St Cycles, New Zealand Avenue, Walton-on-Thames KT12 1QD (01932 221424)

BIKE HIRE: Park Cycle, Roehampton Gate Car Park, Richmond Park SW15 5JR (07050 209249)

ORGANISED RIDES

Sunrise, Dunwich Beach

No.31

DUNWICH DYNAMO

The cult classic night ride from London to the Suffolk coast gets bigger
— and the route gets a tiny bit shorter — every year

The brainchild of Patrick Field and Jez Hastings, the *Dunwich Dynamo* began as an homage to the venerated Paris-Brest-Paris randonnée. Now more than 20 years old, the Dynamo has its own cult reputation, complete with myths and legends. Each edition is bigger than the last; in 2012 an estimated 800 people made it to the beach.

The ride takes place each July on the Saturday night nearest the full moon. It costs nothing; it's not a race; it's not for charity. 'A frivolous, foolish excursion' is how Patrick described it to me, standing on the beach in the morning sunlight wearing an Arsenal shirt, a billowing north African robe and a pair of sandals. That's one way to describe riding 120 miles (193km) through the night to a place that isn't there.

It's a daunting distance for everyone but the most hardened, and sleep deprivation brings its own challenges. But there's often a south-westerly tailwind, and the route is across very gentle country, with only a handful of minor hills. What's more, so many people are riding that encouragement and assistance are never far away. It's a happy night-time cavalcade of every kind of cyclist, from skinny racers looking to reach the beach before dawn to panniered commuters, urban fixies and wizened tourers. I've seen folding bikes, town bikes, tandems, recumbents and even brave souls on a penny farthing and a Boris Bike.

It all begins at the Pub on the Park in London Fields, the first riders drifting away around 8pm.

Under the setting sun, there's a swift escape from London through Epping Forest. Once night falls, all that can be seen is the moon above and a long stream of flashing red lights ahead. In the dead of night there's a half-way 'lunch' stop in a village hall. The queues can be long, and wise riders pack a picnic.

After this come the darkest, coldest hours and sometimes the hardest riding, with the question 'why am I doing this?' looming large. But doubts are dispelled as the sky lightens, black turns to grey, and the scent of the sea fills the air. Enterprising residents along the route man food stalls in their front gardens. In the final push to the coast, weariness gives way to euphoria and a refreshing dip in the sea is the perfect tonic for tired legs before a snooze on the shingle and breakfast in the Flora Café.

Southwark Cyclists organise return coaches, and there are trains from nearby Darsham and from Ipswich, 20 miles down the coast. Alternatively, book a room at the Ship Inn and explore the area (*see* Ride No. 26).

ALSO CONSIDER: If the Dynamo sparks a taste for night rides, check out the *Friday Night Ride to the Coast*, a monthly ride from London to destinations including Southend-on-Sea in Essex, Whitstable in Kent and Felpham in West Sussex.

londonschoolofcycling.co.uk
fnrttc.blogspot.co.uk

No.32

RIDE OF THE FALLING LEAVES

A well-organised, relaxed and good-value early autumn sportive
from Dulwich into Kent and back

———

The continental *cyclosportive*, or sportive, is an increasingly popular entry level form of bike racing. In a traditional bike race, riders try to stay in a tight group and all kinds of team tactics are deployed, but the sportive is an altogether more relaxed affair. Riders set off in small groups and are timed electronically. There are awards based on time, but most people are racing against themselves, or not racing at all – just enjoying a day's ride with friends along a clearly marked, well-marshalled route, with food and drinks provided.

There's sometimes a tie-in with a charity, but sportives are usually organised by sports event companies, and the cost of entry reflects their commercial slant. The biggest, most prestigious and most expensive (up to £60) are held on closed roads, allowing use of the full width of the road with no worries about motor traffic. At the other end of the spectrum are the sportives on open roads organised by amateur cycling clubs, often as fundraisers.

The *Ride of the Falling Leaves* falls squarely into the latter category. Held in early October and organised by the Dulwich Paragon cycling club, it is a relaxed event with 110km (68-mile) and 80km (50-mile) options. Both begin with a lap around the historic Herne Hill Velodrome, which hosted track cycling events in the 1948 Olympics and has recently been resurfaced. Out on the roads, the route heads south through leafy, well-heeled Dulwich, up the hill to Crystal Palace and out through suburban London into the North Downs. After a white-knuckle descent from the

Downs, riders cross over the M25 motorway and ride around the gently rolling valley of the River Eden (*see* Ride No. 3) before turning back north for a series of short, tough climbs – Sundridge Hill being the killer blow – then past the private airport at Biggin Hill and into London, finishing at the clubhouse of the Dulwich Cricket Club. The £20 entry fee somehow covers route maps, timing chips, signage, feed stops, support vans, and hot food and a pint at the end. All the volunteer effort by club members means there's even enough left over for a donation to local charities.

Some aspects of the sportive make me uneasy: high and ever-increasing entry fees, heavy-handed commercial and charity branding and the long distances many riders drive to get to the start. It all seems so much unnecessary distraction from the simple pleasure of a bike ride in the countryside. But the Ride of the Falling Leaves retains its local flavour and thanks to all the volunteers it remains a very well-organised, sociable, accessible and challenging ride. In my three attempts, a gold-standard time of four hours has always just eluded me. Maybe next time.

ALSO CONSIDER: Other sportives worth looking up are Catford Cycling Club's *Hell of the Ashdown* (usually at the end of January), the *Sussex Puncheur* (usually in March) and the *Chiltern Hundred* (usually at the end of May).

dulwichparagon.com
britishcycling.org.uk/sportives

Emitremmus 2012

256

www.stevenagectc.org.uk

ctc
working for cycling

END OF SUMMERTIME AUDAX

Audax is one of the oldest, and oddest, of cycling's subcultures, encompassing a range of events from pleasurable rides for mere mortals to ultra-endurance challenges

———

In the late 19th century bicycles were expensive, the preserve of those with money and time – but they were also the fastest things on the road. In Britain, France and Italy, groups of cyclists began organising timed challenges over set distances, usually around 200km (124 miles) in 14 hours, or approximately sunrise to sunset. No mean feat on the bicycles and roads of the times. One Italian group took the name Audax Italiano, from the Latin *audax* for 'daring' or 'audacious'. In France, Henri Desgrange, founder of the Tour de France, borrowed their name and codified a set of rules.

Audax combines elements of touring and racing into something quite unlike either. An audax (randonnée or brevet are other names) is a group ride on a set route, with a time limit – but it's not a race, and times are not recorded. There is an element of self-sufficiency: with no arrows showing the way, riders navigate from a route sheet with turn-by-turn instructions, checking in at control points on the way to have their brevet cards stamped. It can seem a little daunting to the uninitiated, but it's a friendly world, and new riders are always welcomed. Today there are long and even international rides, but there are also audaxes of much more manageable distances.

Stevenage CTC's annual ride to mark the end of British Summer Time is one of the latter, and a great introduction to the world of audax. Riders choose either a 100km (62-mile) or a shorter 67km (42-mile) route over the quiet, rolling countryside between Stevenage in Hertfordshire and the pretty medieval town of Saffron Walden in Essex. The control points have plenty of refreshments: in 2012, the morning control was in the garden of a tea shop offering delicious homemade sausage rolls and jam doughnuts, and the afternoon control in a village hall where the local Women's Institute were serving teas and homemade cakes.

All kinds of people ride: old and young, fast and slow, everyone at their own pace. With about 500 people taking part, it's easy to tag along with a group to make navigation easier, and there are plenty of technical wizards around who seem very happy to help solve any mechanical problems along the way. At an entry price of £7, the ride is much better value than the commercial sportives (*see* Ride No. 32) and charity rides that have proliferated recently. Who knows, a short ride out in rural Hertfordshire could be the beginning of a journey that leads one day to riding the 1,200km (746-mile) audax from Paris to Brest and back.

ALSO CONSIDER: Other good introductions to audaxing are *Up the Uts* in north Essex and east Hertfordshire (usually in March) and *Watership Down* in Hampshire (usually in January). The Audax UK website lists hundreds of rides a year, across all distances, all over the country.

stevenagectc.org.uk
aukweb.net

Churchend

No. 34

FOULNESS ISLAND BIKE RIDE

A once-a-year chance to ride a bike around an Essex island that is one of the most inaccessible places in southern England

———

G.K. Chesterton observed that 'Britain is not so much an island as an archipelago; it is at least a labyrinth of peninsulas.' The crinkled coastline of Essex is a staggering 350 miles long, with long-fingered peninsulas, creeks, marshes, miles of shimmering mudflats, and at least 30 tiny islands – more than any other English county. The biggest, Foulness, is England's fourth largest island, and also the most secretive.

The two hundred or so residents of Foulness live in quiet isolation because the island is home to a military research station. For nearly a century the latest in bombs, missiles, grenades, torpedoes and even atomic weapons have been tested here, though it's no longer a nuclear facility. Access is strictly controlled though a little museum that tells the history of the island and its rich wildlife is open to the public for a few hours on the first Sunday of the month during summer. Even so, permission must be sought in advance, and access is only as far as the main village of Churchend.

For a proper nose around, it's worth joining the thousand or so cyclists in Thorpe Bay Rotary Club's mass ride in aid of local charities. Entries are accepted right up to the morning of the ride and it begins at the primary school in Great Wakering, the last mainland town before the bridge across to the island. The bridge was built in 1922; before that, access was by boat or the Broomway, a 6-mile long tidal causeway across Maplin Sands.

Once on the island, there's a gentle ride on flat, empty roads across the marshes to Churchend, where the tiny village shop and post office serves refreshments. Beyond, the ride continues inland on lanes and a stretch of unsurfaced road through farmland, past abandoned houses and the island's other small village, Courtsend.

The island's wildlife was here long before the boffins set up shop, and pays no heed to the MOD's restrictions. The name Foulness means 'promontory of the wild birds', and the marshes and mudflats are a bird-spotter's paradise. In winter, migratory species swell the avian population to more than 100,000.

The human population peaked in the mid-19th century, with 751 residents recorded in the 1871 census. Since then it's been a long, slow decline: the last pub closed in 2010 and the church, with its slightly leaning spire, is also closed. With signs of abandonment everywhere, there's something wonderful about the sight of so many brightly coloured cyclists of all ages on bikes of every kind, enjoying a sunny afternoon spin and the rare chance to see one of the strangest, least visited corners of southern England.

ALSO CONSIDER: Another volunteer-run island ride is the *Isle of Wight Randonnée*. There are two distances to choose from, 62 or 31 miles (100km or 50km), no entry fee and no need to pre-register. You can ride from any point in a circle in either direction, stopping in church halls, where tea, squash and homemade cakes are served.

thorpebayrotaryevents.co.uk
cycleisland.co.uk

No.35

LONDON TO BRIGHTON

There's something very satisfying about riding from the city to the sea, and Brighton is London's nearest seaside destination; the journey through Surrey and Sussex is also the country's oldest organised ride

———

The very first pedal 'velocipedes', made in France in the mid-1860s, were rough, heavy machines of wood and iron, with the pedals attached to the front wheel. They hit the headlines in Britain in 1869 when three men held a race from London to Brighton, the winner, John Mayall, completing the 51-mile journey in 'about' 12 hours. It wasn't very much faster than walking, but the friends were celebrated because everyone sensed that this was the start of a new era of personal mobility. This race to the sea inaugurated Britain's very first cycling boom. In the years that followed, the Brighton Road became a mainstay of recreational riding and one of the most popular routes out of the capital.

Then, on May 1st 1976, little over a century later, a London–Brighton cycling rally promised 'a scenic and leisurely ride from the city to the sea'. It was organised by the Friends of the Earth, with hand-drawn flyers proclaiming 'More Bicycles → Cleaner Cities'. By this time the original Brighton Road was a busy dual carriageway, so the ride took a more circuitous route. Around 60 people set out; only half finished. The following year the route was shortened, and the infamous Ditchling Beacon climb was included. In the 1980s, the British Heart Foundation took the event under its wing, seeing its potential as a charity challenge ride – a new kind of cycling event, with riders raising money through sponsorship. In 2012 some 27,000 people took part in the BHF ride. It's now so popular that there are nighttime and off-road versions as well as the main ride. Other charities have joined the bandwagon, organising their own rides along the same route.

At 54 miles (87km), it's just long enough to give those relatively new to cycling a genuine sense of achievement, but not so long that there's any real danger of not finishing. There are only three significant climbs; the last, over Ditchling Beacon on the South Downs, is the toughest. Congestion is a real problem on the main ride, and Ditchling Beacon gets so crowded that most end up pushing their bikes. But the view from the top is truly magnificent, and then it's downhill all the way to the seafront at Brighton.

Anyone can ride from London to Brighton: it needn't be for charity in an organised ride. The very ambitious might ride back, perhaps over Devil's Dyke and through the Surrey Hills, the route of the annual Ditchling Devil audax.

ALSO CONSIDER: I'm not the biggest fan of charity rides, which can give the impression that cycling is done for virtue rather than pleasure; but if they can tempt the hesitant to take up cycling, the BHF Oxford to Cambridge ride at 88 miles (142km), with shorter segments also available, and the 60-mile (97km) London to Cambridge ride in aid of Breakthrough Breast Cancer are good events.

bhf.org.uk
breakthrough.org.uk

Soho

South Bank

MIDSUMMER MADNESS

Ride quiet London streets on the shortest night of the year,
and greet the rising sun at the start of the longest day

The summer solstice is the shortest night of the year and celebrated throughout the world, from druids and revellers gathered at the Stonehenge and Avebury stone circles to people in Baltic and Scandinavian countries, where midsummer is the biggest holiday of the year after Christmas. Solstice celebrations are one of the oldest and most universal of all human traditions, known to date back as far as Neolithic times. One of best places in London to watch the sun rise on midsummer's day is the top of Primrose Hill, which offers a fine view across the city's ever-changing skyline towards the first light in the east.

In the dead of night, as the city sleeps, its streets are largely empty of traffic, making midsummer night a pleasantly rewarding time to explore by bicycle. Southwark Cyclists, one of the borough groups of the London Cycling Campaign, organise a free, turn-up-and-go night ride through the city. It starts at Cutty Sark Gardens, on the banks of the Thames at Greenwich, near where east meets west at the Greenwich Meridian. The ride sets off at two in the morning heading west to a second meeting point by London Bridge, where more riders join the crowd. From there it's over the Thames, and a magical ride through the dark and eerily deserted streets of the Square Mile, past the churches of Wren and Hawksmoor and into the West End. Soho is buzzing at any time of day or night, and a coffee stop at Bar Italia on Frith Street helps to keep the eyelids open before riding through Fitzrovia, around a surprisingly darkened Regent's Park and up the steep climb up Primrose Hill. There's always a good crowd at the top waiting for the sun to appear at around a quarter to five, away over the towers of Canary Wharf. After that, head back over the river to the South Bank for breakfast at a greasy spoon café: sleep deprivation never felt so good.

ALSO CONSIDER: *The Bridges*, organised by the London Fixed Gear and Single Speed Forum, is a 22-mile (35km) nighttime traverse of London, crossing each of the 19 bridges over the Thames that are open to bikes between Tower Bridge in the east and Kew Bridge in the west. It takes place at least twice a year, in alternate directions, east-west and west-east.

Southwark Cyclists also organise *Locks, Docks and One Smoking Ferry*, a turn-up-and-go ride that explores the north and south banks of the Thames including a trip on the Woolwich Ferry. Best on summer evenings.

The *London Classic* is a popular daytime ride around the capital, held in early April, that promises a 35-mile (56km) route featuring 'bone-shaking cobbles and lung-busting hills'. The ride is free to enter, but registration is required.

southwarkcyclists.org.uk
lfgss.com
thelondonclassic.org

BEFORE YOU GO
PRACTICALITIES

——

ROUTES AND MAPS

The rides in this book range in length from less than 10 miles (16km) to more than 60 miles (96km) but most are around the 30-mile (48km) mark, which is a good distance for a leisurely day ride for most people, or a half-day ride for the more energetic. I've deliberately refrained from adding timings to the rides, as it's far better to ride at your own pace than somebody else's.

The maps in the book are sketches, best used in combination with a good paper map, e.g. the Ordnance Survey's 1:50,000 Landranger series. They are costly but can be borrowed from most public libraries or go to bing.com/maps to view and print online.

Maps, route sheets with instructions and GPS navigation files are available for each ride online. The web address for these is given in the details at the end of the ride.

GPS NAVIGATION

GPS navigation is less good for exploring and improvising than a paper map but it excels when following a preplanned route, assuming your batteries don't run out. For each ride in the book (except the organised group rides) the web page above includes a GPX file that can be downloaded for use in a GPS navigation device or smartphone. For plotting new routes for GPS navigation, bikehike.co.uk is a great resource.

TAKE THE TRAIN

All the rides are accessible by train on direct services from central London. For £30 a year, a Network Railcard reduces most fares in the region by a third for up to four people travelling together. GroupSave tickets also offer big savings for groups

of three and four. Most train companies restrict bicycle access on trains that go into and out of London during peak weekday commuting times, when most trains are at their busiest. Sometimes it makes sense to travel to and return from different stations on the same line; just buy a return ticket to the furthest station.

ANY KIND OF BIKE

The rides in this book can be ridden on any bike that's in good mechanical order and the right size for the rider. Low gears make climbing hills much less daunting. Tyre choice makes a huge difference to the sensation of riding a bike; good-quality tyres between 28mm and 37mm in diameter are a sensible all-round choice for a fast and comfortable ride. Unless it's the middle of a heatwave, mudguards should be considered an essential item. It's one thing being rained on from above, it's quite another having a jet of mucky water sprayed up at you from below.

LIGHTS, LOCKS & LUGGAGE

When riding in the dark, a set of lights is a legal requirement. Good lights are well worth the money and modern battery-powered LED lights are very bright and last for a long time. On dark country lanes, supplementing lights with reflective material is a good idea.

In the countryside, a lock is often unnecessary but can be a good precaution, especially if you plan to leave your bicycle unattended for any length of time. A small cable is enough to deter an opportunist, but in cities or large towns, where professional bike thieves may be lurking, it makes sense to pack a heavier, more secure lock. A single lock can be enough to secure several bikes.

Money, a basic tool kit, a snack and a mobile phone can be stuffed into a very small rucksack, bumbag or in the rear pockets of a cycling jersey. Anything heavier is more comfortable if carried on the bicycle itself, in either a handlebar bag, a saddle bag or a pannier.

CLOTHING AND SHOES

In spite of the images of Lycra-clad racers presented in magazines and on television, the overwhelming majority of people in the world who ride bikes do so in perfectly ordinary clothing. There's nothing wrong with indulging a taste for the latest cycling gear and donning a cycling uniform of one kind or another, but the reality is that whatever clothing is comfortable going for a walk in the park will be fine for riding a bike in the countryside for a few hours.

Tight jeans and raised seams can become a source of discomfort if worn on on longer rides. Padded shorts or underwear provide extra comfort if needed. In heavy rain, thick cotton and denim are quickly waterlogged and will take longer to dry out than wool and synthetic fibres like Lycra. Riding in the rain isn't much fun but lightweight,

breathable waterproof fabrics like Gore-Tex Paclite are wonderful when compared to old-style plastic pac-a-macs. Many cyclists – including weight-conscious racers – still swear by light-weight nylon capes that keep the rain out while allowing air to flow underneath, thus avoiding the 'boil -in-the-bag' syndrome of a fully sealed garment. For night rides and camping trips, a few extra layers are a good idea, as well as a warm hat. In cold weather, thick, windproof gloves keep fingers nice and warm.

Cycling-specific shoes are unnecessary for all but the most speed-conscious racers. Big, flat pedals with good grip allow almost any type of shoe to be worn, and people have cycled many miles in sandals, flip flops, espadrilles, loafers, wellington boots as well as high-heeled sneakers and blue suede shoes. Comfort and grip are the most important considerations.

WHEN THINGS GO WRONG

Compared with running a car, the costs of maintaining a bicycle, even if all the work is done by a bike shop, is tiny. Assuming the bicycle is in generally good mechanical order, the skills and tools necessary to mend a puncture and fix a dropped chain are enough to guarantee self-sufficiency on day rides. A truly worst-case scenario means phoning for a taxi to the nearest train station.

A basic on-the-road repair kit consists of the following:

- Tyre levers, a pump and a couple of spare inner tubes
- A puncture repair kit
- The screwdrivers and Allen keys needed to remove wheels, adjust brakes and tighten your rack, mudguard fittings and seat-post clamp
- Cable ties (zip ties) come in a handy and a bungy is useful for securing bikes on trains

Learning a little about how a bike works not only saves money but comes with a warm glow of self-sufficiency. Some tasks are best left to a professional, but the basics are easily mastered. If there's nobody around to give a hands-on lesson, buy a bike maintenance book or look online for instructional videos, for example, those by Patrick Field of the London School of Cycling available at at *madegood.org*.

RIDING SAFE & SOUND
Riding a safe distance (at least 1.5m/5ft) from the roadside and any parked cars is much safer than hugging the kerb. Making eye contact with other road users helps everyone get along. If wearing a helmet, make sure it's undamaged and fastened securely.

On roads, it is cyclists that suffer most from the boorish attitude that 'might makes right' and so we should be at pains to preserve the civility of traffic-free paths shared with walkers, skaters and horse-riders. Be aware that other people are out enjoying themselves too and may not be paying full attention. Approach horse riders with caution and a verbal greeting to let the beast know that you're human.

When leading group rides with slower or less experienced cyclists, rather than speed off and leave the group trailing in your wake, aim to ride at a pace that's no faster than the slowest riders can manage comfortably. It's a good idea to have a more experienced cyclist ride as a back-marker.

CLUBS & ORGANISATIONS
Membership of the Cyclists Touring Club, the London Cycling Campaign or your local cycling group not only helps these worthy organisations campaign on behalf of cyclists, it also brings benefits like discounts in bike shops, member magazines, third party insurance and free legal advice in the very unlikely event of an accident. Most CTC and LCC local groups have full programmes of free or very nearly free rides, which are a great way of discovering new places and meeting new people, with an experienced ride leader taking care of all the navigation and planning tea and lunch stops.

There are also strong communities of cyclists online. The Yet Another Cycling Forum (*www.yacf.co.uk*) leans towards touring and commuting while the London Fixed Gear and Single Speed Forum (*lfgss.com*) has been at the beating heart of British urban bike culture since 2007. Both are lively places to look for advice, to find out about rides, routes and events, all leavened by varying degrees of friendly banter.

The National Trust and English Heritage maintain hundreds of amazing properties across the country, but entry fees can be high if you're just making a fleeting visit while out on a bike ride. If you're the kind of person who enjoys visiting historic buildings and sumptuous gardens, an annual membership makes sense and all funds help contribute to the upkeep of their wonderful properties. Similarly, the Royal Society for the Protection of Birds, the Wildlife Trusts and Plantlife are member-funded charities that do important work conserving and restoring the natural environment and maintain some superb nature reserves.

Finally, tuning in to The Bike Show, the weekly radio show I present on London's Resonance FM, also available as a podcast via iTunes and at *thebikeshow.net*, is another way to immerse yourself in all things bicycle.

EPILOGUE

THESE ROADS ARE OUR ROADS

——

There was a time, well within living memory, when every road in Britain was welcoming to cyclists. In 1949 British people travelled more miles by bicycle than than they did by car; well into the 1960s, many cyclists thought nothing of riding their bikes long distances on main roads. Back then, motor vehicles were smaller and slower, and most importantly of all, there were a lot fewer of them. Times have changed. While there is a measurable increase in the number of people travelling by bike, particularly in London, car use has risen five-fold since 1960 and cycling seems set to remain a minority mode of travel. That minority status has dramatically reduced the number of roads that are realistically viable for cycling.

Cyclists are now effectively denied access to A-roads, the routes that follow the best, most direct lines through the countryside and avoid the biggest hills, because riding along a busy highway with a stream of huge lorries and fast cars whizzing past is only for the brave or the foolhardy. A very few main roads do now have rudimentary cycle tracks alongside; while these can help to take the fear out of riding, they tend to be intermittent, narrow and poorly surfaced, and the motor-dominated environment remains just as noisy and unpleasant.

A couple of decades ago B-roads, the secondary network of less busy connecting roads between medium-sized towns and villages, were still a good bet for cycling. But these days it's a much more mixed picture, and most B-roads are quite hostile for cycling or walking. They are too narrow for cars to overtake easily but are wide enough that people drive too fast for comfort. This is why I always head for the tens of thousands of miles of quiet, unclassified roads that thread their way across the countryside, the lost lanes that are a joy to ride and are the main focus of this book. But I'd hate to see cycling confined to lost lanes forever.

The bicycle has been with us for more than a century, and nobody has yet invented a more efficient way to travel. Driving a car uses 50 to 80 times as much energy as making the same journey by bike. A cyclist moves three times as fast as someone walking, for the same expenditure of energy. As more people rediscover the pleasure of riding a bike as a pastime and for sport, they may also consider using it for everyday journeys like going to work, doing a quick shop or taking the kids to school. We may yet reclaim the roads that earlier, more fortunate generations of cyclists took for granted. We may yet convince our governments to add fast, smooth and direct cycle tracks on the same direct routes as busy roads, as they have in the Netherlands. We may yet persuade them to lower speed limits where people live, work and play. We may yet reshape our towns and cities around living instead of around driving.

It is a monumental task that will take time, effort, and the continued dedication of organisations like Sustrans, the Campaign for Better Transport, the Cyclists' Touring Club, the London Cycling Campaign, the Cycling Embassy of Great Britain and hundreds of local campaigns around the country. But it can be done. Every time you ride a bike, you're adding another voice to the growing chorus demanding that our roads be made safe, pleasant and people-friendly places once again. Together, we'll get there.

254

Lost Lanes
36 Glorious
Bike Rides in
Southern England

Words and photos:
Jack Thurston

Cover illustrations:
Andrew Pavitt

Design and layout:
Oliver Mann
Marcus Freeman
Karen Willcox

Editor:
Candida Frith-Macdonald

Proofreader:
Michael Lee

Production:
Daniel Start

Published by:
Wild Things Publishing Ltd
Bath, United Kingdom

Distributed by:
Central Books Ltd
99 Wallis Road
London, E9 5LN
Tel +44 (0)845 458 9911
orders@centralbooks.com

wildthingspublishing.com

lostlanes.thebikeshow.net

Photographs and maps
All photographs © Jack Thurston except: p.37 (top and bottom left) © Daniel
Start, p. 192 © Tim Dawson, and p.244 (bottom) © British Heart Foundation (all
with permission); p.81 (top left) © shirokazan, p.81 (top right and bottom) ©
Stefan Czapski, p. 244 (top left) © Remy Sharp, p.244 (top right) © Neil
Cummings, p.246 (top) © Craig Morey, p.246 (bottom left) © Sean Jackson, p.246
(bottom right) © elyob (all CC-BY-SA).
Map data © OpenStreetMap contributors.
Maps generated using bikehike.co.uk and gpsvisualizer.com.

Acknowledgements
I'm grateful to the friends, family and listeners to The Bike Show who've joined me
on the rides, offered advice and helped check routes. Thanks to Hannah Boyton,
Joff Verby, Anna Gudaniec, Matthew Walters, Fenn Kiddle, Tim Dawson, Simone
Lewis, Alan Ball, Ed Wright, Pete Devery, Bill Gentry, Nick Cobbing, Harry Adès,
Shahla Shah, Sylvie Adès, Rémy Adès, Jean-Marie Orhan, John Armour, Dick
Vincent, Lu Everett, Lionel Birnie, Helen Jukes, Julia Wylie, Ruby Wright, Lazlo
Miodownik, Nick Appleton, Paul Bommer, Sara, Hildy and Gus Bredemear,
Andrew Jeffery, Jason Morris, Peter Reed, Ben Flower, Matthew Burton, Richard
Hamilton, Thomas Steven, Hugh Grainger, Richard Craven, Alberto Contreras and
Andrea Casalotti. Thank you, Patrick Field and Grant Petersen, for showing the
way.

This book has been made by an all-star team. My thanks to Marcus and Oliver for
the superb design work, to Andrew for the stunning illustration, to Michael for his
eagle eyes and to Candida, the perfect stoker (and, occasionally, pilot) on an epic
tandem tour. The responsibility for all mistakes and wrong turns is mine alone. A
thousand thanks to Daniel, for the encouragement, advice and many years of
cycling fun. Greatest thanks to Sarah, my beloved companion on the biggest
journey of all, by bike and otherwise.

Ride No. 6 is dedicated to the memory of Barry Mason, a true pioneer.